KIERKEGAARD'S ROMANTIC LEGACY

TWO THEORIES OF THE SELF

D1500881

KIERKEGAARD'S ROMANTIC LEGACY

TWO THEORIES OF THE SELF

Anoop Gupta

University of Ottawa Press

The University of Ottawa Press gratefully acknowledges the support extended to its publishing programme by the Canada Council for the Arts and the University of Ottawa.

We also acknowledge with gratitude the support of the Government of Canada through its Book Publishing Industry Development Program for our publishing activities.

National Library of Canada Cataloguing in Publication

Gupta, Anoop, 1969-
    Kierkegaard's romantic legacy : two theories of the self / Anoop Gupta.

(Philosophica, ISSN 1480-4670)

Includes bibliographical references and index.

ISBN-13: 978-0-7766-0616-3
ISBN-10: 0-7766-0616-6

    1. Kierkegaard, Søren, 1813-1855. 2. Self (Philosophy). I. Title. II. Series: Collection Philosophica.

B4378.S4G86 2005   198'.9   C2005-906294-0

Canada word mark

University of
Ottawa Press

Cover art: Heather Horton
Cover design: Laura Brady
Interior design and typesetting: Brad Horning
Copyeditor: Marie Clausén
Proofreader: Stephanie VanderMeulen

Published by the University of Ottawa Press, 2005
542 King Edward Avenue, Ottawa, Ontario K1N 6N5
press@uottawa.ca / www.uopress.uottawa.ca

Printed and bound in Canada

This book is dedicated to the individual soul,
wherever it may find some solace, in the age of reason.

If I go insane, please don't put your wires in my brain.
—Pink Floyd
"If," *Atom Heart Mother*

Contents

Kierkegaard's Theological Self

The Sociological Self

Some Consequences For Practice

PREFACE

QUITE SOME TIME HAS ELAPSED between my writing this manuscript and the bringing of it to print. I began research on it in 1996, while a master's committee was contemplating my thesis. I continued to revise it after my doctorate, ten years after its initial inception. I am pleased it was allowed to take this amount of time, as my ideas germinated, morphed, and crystallized as time passed. I wanted to deliver my most recent, and clearest, statement on selfhood.

Although generally a committed follower of naturalism and realism, I renounce reductionism (which some types of realism are thought to entail) if it eliminates, for instance, the self. In attempting to avoid reductionism, I follow the pragmatism of Hilary Putnam.

If one disputes the extreme naturalist contention that there is no self, one must in doing so present a suggestion as to what we are. I consider several authors, whom I locate, roughly, in the romantic reaction against the Enlightenment, and which have something to say about the nature of the self. Furthermore, I emphasize, as a pragmatist must, that there is a relevance to practice for holding a certain conception of the self.

The problem of reductionism is a natural consequence of the intellectual revolutions that began in the seventeenth century. The Enlightenment, for instance, was an intellectual revolution which held that reason—by which the enlightened meant something like the critical spirit of scientific inquiry—could solve humanity's problems, be they medical, economic, social, and so on.

The romantic tradition reacted against the Enlightenment. It was not, however, totally at odds with the Enlightenment, but can in retrospect be seen to occupy a place beside it. For instance, the enlightened and the romantic, like their cognitive heirs the reductionist and anti-reductionist, respectively, need each other to develop and nuance their views.

I have as indicated in the title of this work, wished to emphasize the importance of the romantic tradition in the development of intellectual thought of the West, and how, more specifically, it has contributed to a discourse about the self. I hope that cognitive scientists, interested in more than the physiological side of the story, will profit from this discussion on the self.

Scholars of Kierkegaard may find that some of his concepts—for example, choice, faith, subjectivity, and so on—are not scrutinized in this my exegesis of his writings as much as they may require in order to have their complexities fully explored. Nevertheless, these deficiencies are tolerable, I believe, as my stated focus is his theory of the self (and some of its legacy).

Furthermore, I have avoided as much as possible Kierkegaard's polemic against Hegel. Kierkegaard was no authority on Hegel (it is unlikely he read his writings). Kierkegaard was not as far from Hegel's thought as he may have wished, either in terms of his dialectical style or content. German idealism was, after all, an expression of Romanticism in that country, where the self was conceived, literally, in relation to everything. As Plato put it, in the *Phaedrus*, "And do you think that you can know the nature of the soul intelligently without knowing the nature of the whole?"

ACKNOWLEDGEMENTS

I thank Nicholas Griffin, of the Bertrand Russell Research Centre, McMaster University, for assisting me with access to the collection at Mills Memorial Library. His continued interest was a source of encouragement, and noteworthy, as my book is far removed from the Russell Project. I thank Andrew Brook, Director of The Institute of Interdisciplinary Studies at Carleton University, for sharing his encyclopaedic knowledge, and passion, for the philosophy of mind. I thank Mathieu Marion at UQAM, Peter McCormick, from the University of Liechtenstein, Barry Allen, Gary B. Madison, both of McMaster University, Martha Hussain, the Aristotle scholar, and Harry Hunt, the theorist of the self, both of Brock University. I gratefully acknowledge the generous support of CanWrite.ca, and specifically Mohan Juneja, its coordinator. CanWrite.ca is an organization dedicated to assisting Canadian writers, a group I am fortunate enough to belong to. Finally, I thank the three anonymous referees for their scrutiny of the text and, for his persistent support, the assistant editor at the University of Ottawa Press, Eric Nelson. Finally, I acknowledge Marie Clausén, managing editor at the University of Ottawa Press and also my copy-editor, who did a first-rate job.

DOCUMENTATION

In "Kierkegaard's Theological Self" I refer to "supplements"; when I do so I am referring to the additional sections added by the editors of Kierkegaard's texts, called "supplements" in those texts. A "supplement" will contain, for instance, excerpts from Kierkegaard's journal entries, unpublished manuscripts, and so on, which I draw upon to build my case. Where Kierkegaard expounds a point that resonated from the Bible, I have attempted to refer to the corresponding quotation within the text, citing the book.

SEARCH FOR
THE KIERKEGAARDIAN SELF

WE NEED TO UNDERSTAND WHY we should consider Kierkegaard's theory of the self, and how I intend to develop it. In what follows, we shall grasp the importance of investigating Kierkegaard's theory, and how I shall proceed.

Historically, the romantics reacted against the imposition of reason, by which they meant something akin to the naturalist methods of science. Scientism can be understood as an extreme form of naturalism. A. Brook and R. Stainton, in a useful account of the variety of naturalisms, write of the extreme version:

> *Stronger naturalism* is the idea that philosophical problems about knowledge and the mind (and almost everything else) are really scientific ones and can be adequately answered by using only the methods of science, natural science in particular...***Strongest naturalism* is the idea that one accepts stronger naturalism but goes one step further. It holds that *neuroscience* is the only justifiable approach to cognition.** [Emphasis mine.][1]

For the strongest naturalist, there is likely no self, only biochemical happening.[2]

In the enlightened tradition, scientism has had many guises. We have alternately been considered the totality of our experiences; the end product of socialization; a result of our particular historical or biological situation. According to this tradition, there is nothing under the surface, there is no soul, no "real me." Scientism's greatest challenge to theorists of the self is its denial that there is such an entity.

Furthermore, some extreme naturalists and existentialists claim the self is a tabula rasa. According to the strongest naturalists, our bodies are simply biochemical machines that allow imprinting, while according to existentialists, we are the results of acts of will.

G. Pence remarks:

> [A] central principle of existentialism [...] holds that the essence of any human being is completely determined by the free choices made by that already-existing person. It denies that God or anything else created a

human nature that makes humans a certain way. For existentialists, what
we know as "human nature" is not something we inherit but is merely a
generalization we make from millions of ways of acting that people have
chosen and hence, could have chosen differently. [3]

Also, to claim the self is nothing but its (personal and social) history, without
qualifications, leads to cultural relativism.[4] If there is no universal archetype
to which we ought to conform, human nature is denied. Søren Kierkegaard,
upon my reading, does not subscribe to the slogan "existence precedes essence";
Kierkegaard would have rejected existentialism. His view is closer to Aristotle's
than, say, to Jean-Paul Sartre's.

The Romantic movement can be said to stem from two points of conjecture,
namely, (1) the rejection of scientism, and (2) the assumption of an ethic where
we find our fulfilment in the world alone. Kierkegaard embraced the former
notion while rejecting the latter, but can nontheless be considered a romantic,
as the former point is of some significance.

In the first part of this book, I develop a notion of a theological self from the
writings of Kierkegaard. My argument proceeds by citation of textual evidence.
In chapter 1, I set out the existential problem Kierkegaard sees residing in
the self (despair). In chapter 2, I consider Kierkegaard's attempt to solve the
problem, which culminates in the ethical stage of existing. In chapters 3 and 4,
I consider his contention that we find our fulfilment in a relationship to God.
In the interpretive exegesis, one may wish to note, I rarely distinguish between
Kierkegaard and his pseudonyms, and my reason for this conscious blur is the
fact that Kierkegaard himself at times cites his pseudonyms as saying what he
himself wants to say. I explain this at greater length in chapter 5.

In the second part, I introduce sociological accounts of human nature as being
anchored in the world. Human behaviour becomes, for the sociologist, neither
right nor wrong, but functional or non-functional. I trace how a theological
view of the self gave way to a social one, in the writings of, for example,
Rousseau, Durkheim, and, more recently, Winnicott. A formerly ethical issue,
such as becoming a virtuous self, has here in various ways been turned into
a social issue.

However, I also attempt to use sociological thought to bring out the hidden
social dimension of Kierkegaard's thought; that is, I use sociological thought
in constructing my Kierkegaardian theory of the self. At the end of chapter 8, I
argue that those sociological efforts considered are not necessarily at odds with
Kierkegaard, but differ by degree. In fact, like Kierkegaard, the sociological
theorists considered can generically be described as being in the romantic
tradition.

We may think it as absurd to locate Kierkegaard in the romantic tradition
because of his asceticism as doing so with Durkheim, because of Kierkegaard's
desire to be scientific. Yet, I contend, they represent different strains within
the romantic tradition. Like William Blake, the archetype of Romanticism,
Kierkegaard, with his discussion of faith, fits within the romantic tradition's
reaction against scientism. Also like Blake, Durkheim was concerned about

the losses we incurred with industrialization. In the context of this study, both Kierkegaard and the sociologists share three things: first, the rejection of scientism (i.e., they have a non-reductive account of the self); second, in their unique ways, they provide a social account of the self, and in so doing offer a critique of the modern world; finally, their accounts of the self are teleological.

Obviously, Kierkegaard differs from sociologists in his emphasis upon the God-relationship. Derivatively, there is a also a difference between the theological and sociological conception of the self in relation to a notion central to the romantic tradition, namely, that the eschatology of the self terminates in a radical individuality, which Kierkegaard embraces and sociologists do not. Yet, I shall not dwell upon the God-relationship as indicating a broader incommensurability between Kierkegaard and the sociologists, since there is much to be gained, as I suggest, by bringing them together. In chapter 8, I argue that the tension between the two notions of where the self finds fulfilment— alone (with God) or in a community—can be reconciled, to a significant extent, along the lines of Winnicott. The commonality, I shall argue, is to be found in Winnicott's notion of interdependence. Concisely put, a Kierkegaardian would say that we require a social vehicle in order to be independent at all, and in order to find fulfillment.

In the third part of the book, I consider the practical consequences of adopting the romantic conceptions of the self as discussed. In chapters 9 and 10, I have chosen two examples, those of suicide and schizophrenia, to illustrate how historically the theological conception of the self has had a different effect on practice than the sociological one. In chapter 11, however, by considering the thought of A. Adler, L. Binswanger, R. May, and R. D. Laing, I draw out what uniform consequences to practice have been obtained from the generically Kierkegaardian conception of the self.

I do not claim that Adler, Binswanger, May, or Laing (or J. Hillman for that matter) actually read Kierkegaard or the sociological thinkers here considered, and developed their practice based on such studies. Biographically, that could perhaps be determined; but investigating the specific sources of each individual thinker goes beyond the more general point I aim to make. Namely, that it is the bits and pieces of the thought of people like Kierkegaard, filtered through the romantic tradition, that has made the work of the existential psychiatrists possible.

Finally, in chapter 12, I provide three conclusions about the Kierkegaardian self. My intention is not to merely rehearse Kierkegaard's theory of the self but to develop it in relation to criticisms. I shall, in what follows, use the designation "Kierkegaardian," referring (unless the context suggests otherwise) to the theory of the self developed in this work. My Kierkegaardian account of the self, or its application, is not intended to be a faithful (re)creation of what Kierkegaard himself may have thought.

My account differs from many contemporary theories about the self. The Kierkegaardian self is metaphysical. The authors I consider contend, specifically, that there is such a thing as a self and that it has a nature.[5] I shall provide a contribution to theories of the self by looking to the little-remarked upon writings (in this context) of Kierkegaard. I shall also criticize and amend his view in light of a sociological alternative. Tracing the legacy of several theories of the self, all of which I locate within the Romantic movement, is an historical project; yet I suggest the Kierkegaardian self as developed here has contemporary relevance.

All the views presented in this study are anti-reductionist. I do not specifically argue against the strongest form of naturalism; I merely refer to it as the backdrop against which the romantic views, discussed here, react. Since my goal is to develop a Kierkegaardian theory of the self, I avoid delving into all contemporary criticisms of reductionism.[6]

Furthermore, while not all naturalists are prey to scientism, for the purpose of elucidation, I bypass views in cognitive science and medical psychiatry that would be consistent with the authors I consider. Also, bringing Kierkegaard's thought into dialogue with practice, without considering, for example, the most recent literature surrounding reductionism in medical psychiatry, is justified. I attempt to illustrate the suggestion that the Kierkegaardian self is relevant to practice today by considering some contemporary romantics, for instance, the existential psychiatrists.

As Heraclitus cautioned, however, "You would not find out the boundaries of the soul though you travelled every road, so deep is its *logos*."[7] There are limitations to how far we can detail what constitutes human nature. Yet, it is awareness of limitations that defines the accuracy of knowledge.

❧ 1 ❧

KIERKEGAARD'S THEOLOGICAL SELF

⚘ 1 ⚘

STRUCTURE OF THE SELF

FOR KIERKEGAARD, though we must make our selves, there is a right way and a wrong way to do it. His understanding of self fits well with the ethos of Aristotelian metaphysics, where *what a thing is* is defined by *what it is meant to be*. I shall argue, therefore, that the proper perspective for understanding the metaphysics of Kierkegaard's notion of the self is that of teleology.

There is generally a lack of appreciation of how traditional Kierkegaard's seemingly iconoclastic theory of the self is. In this chapter, we will see that he does in fact retain a metaphysical conception of the self.

Below, I consider Kierkegaard's definition of selfhood, and what goads us to develop despair. Then I explore his notion of despair, specifically why he thinks it to be necessary for human development.

DESPAIR

Anti-Climacus, the pseudonym used to write *Sickness unto Death*, provides valuable insight in what the self was for Kierkegaard. Anti-Climacus says, "A self is spirit. But what is spirit? Spirit is the self."[1] Anti-Climacus also remarks, "The self is not a relation but the relation's relating to itself. A human being is a synthesis of the infinite and the finite, of the temporal and the eternal, of freedom and necessity."[2] According to Kierkegaard, the self is a synthesis, such that we cannot have the conception of infinitude without the finite, of freedom without necessity, of the eternal without the temporal. For him, each item is metaphysically related to its opposite. There is also the further relation that relates to itself. "This relation is the positive third, and this is the self."[3]

For Kierkegaard, the self is reflection. Anti-Climacus says that imagination also is reflection. It is by imagining that we in fact represent ourselves to ourselves. We do not simply look in a mirror and say, "yes, there I am." We have a certain conception of ourselves as lazy, courageous, worthless, independent, and so on. The self represents itself as possibility. Anti-Climacus says, "The imagination is the whole of reflection's possibility; and the intensity of this medium is the possibility of the self's intensity."[4] If we are to admit that we imagine ourselves in a particular way, it is clear that part of this imagining is that of thinking of *what we can be*. Thus we have people who *always knew* they were going to be doctors, lawyers, musicians, or amount to nothing.

Let us reiterate the basic structure of self according to Kierkegaard. It can be said to consist of two opposing poles that stand in relation to one another. The one pole of the self can be called necessity and the other possibility. All other categories could be found to be reduced to or be in kinship with these basic concepts. On the one hand we have temporality, necessity, finitude, and on the other hand, the eternal, possibility, infinitude. The self is not one or the other, but both together in a relation that relates to itself.

When we think of our selves, we could, for example, meditate upon necessity. It is necessary that we eat, that our bodies will die, that we were born, and that we had a particular experience. The past is the paradigm of necessity. I cannot change the past whether my childhood was a happy one or one spent locked in a closet.

Conversely, within certain natural limitations it is quite possible that I could do any number of things in the future; the possible allows me to make the future different from the past. The possible is *what is not yet*, where necessity is *what actually is* (or what has been actualized). If we think of the self as a story, it has a past and a future, and is itself in a state of unfolding.

Kierkegaard concedes that we *become* ourselves. We have the freedom to make certain choices in our lives. Yet, if we are to consider life as the task of becoming ourselves, as Kierkegaard does, failure is a clear risk. Anti-Climacus holds that your life is wasted if you have not become aware of yourself as spirit. There is the possibility that we may not become ourselves; we could rather lose ourselves. Anti-Climacus remarks, "The biggest danger, that of losing ourselves, can pass off in the world as quietly as if it were nothing; every other loss, an arm, a leg, five dollars, a wife, etc. is bound to be noticed."[5] When we lose something tangible, it is obvious; but if we lose ourselves, it is unlikely to be noticed.

Now, let us meditate upon the words *to become ourselves* in more detail. To become ourselves, according to Kierkegaard, is to relate our self to itself.[6] Basically, we can understand Kierkegaard to be affirming human nature, yet the imposition of free will makes living in accordance with our true nature a task. The failure to fulfill the existential task is a sickness, which Kierkegaard calls despair.

Anti-Climacus believes there to be three types of despair, which are all understood as "sickness of the spirit."[7] First, unauthentic despair: being unconscious of having a self. This could be the case if we, for instance, were lost in a crowd. Despair, thus, is even present in those who claim not to have experienced it. "What is rare, the great rarity, is that one should truly not be in despair...it altogether overlooks that the very fact of not being in despair, or not being conscious of being in despair, is itself a form of despair."[8] Anti-Climacus wants us to admit that we can be in despair even when we do not think we are. In fact, he says that "not being in despair may exactly be to be in despair."[9] According to Kierkegaard, unauthentic despair is not functional: it does not aid in the development of the self. For Kierkegaard, to recognize oneself as in despair is to realize that one was always so.

The second type of despair is not wanting to be ourselves, of desiring to be rid of ourselves. The extreme case is, of course, suicide, where we are sick of our self. Anti-Climacus, however, writes:

> On the contrary, the torment of despair is precisely the inability to die... to be sick unto death is to be unable to die, yet not as though there were no hope in life. No, the hopelessness is that even the last hope, death, is gone...When the danger is so great that death has become the hope, then despair is the hopelessness of not even being able to die.[10]

The torment of despair, in its most definite sense, is that with the suffering of life we cannot even die. Anti-Climacus says, "Yet despair is a consumption of the self, but an impotent self-conception not capable of doing what it wants."[11] Despair consumes the self, but never fully, as "he cannot consume himself, cannot be rid of himself, and cannot become nothing. This is the heightened formula for despair, the rising fever in this sickness of the self."[12] Despair, in one sense, is consuming us. Even so, it is not successful in doing so, and this results in the heightening of despair at not being able to rid onseself of one's self; despair falls short of "doing what it wants" and hence despair is retained. Anti-Climacus remarks, "To despair over oneself, in despair to want to be rid of oneself, is the formula for all despair."[13] Whereas physical sickness can or will kill the body, sickness of the soul cannot kill the soul: "despair cannot consume his self, […] this is precisely the torment of contradiction in despair."[14] The self is preserved in despair.

Anti-Climacus says, however, that all forms of despair can be reduced to the third type of despair, "wanting in despair to be oneself."[15] In this case, we may want to be ourselves, yet by trying to invent ourselves, we in vain avoid becoming ourselves. Since the self is always transcending toward the possible, despair comes from the recognition of the end of "the possible": death.

Even the despair of wanting to be ourselves, says Anti-Climacus, can be understood as a mechanism by which we avoid being ourselves. We think "I want to be person X"—Caesar, in Anti-Climacus's example—but all the while we are only avoiding ourselves.

For Kierkegaard, despair represents an imbalance within the dialectics of the self. Anti-Climacus describes the eradication of despair in this way: "In relating to itself and in wanting to be itself, the self is grounded transparently in the power that established it."[16] The power referred to is God. So, by becoming ourselves we set right our position to God. Despair, conversely, amounts to not being ourselves, which for Kierkegaard means not having attained a relation to the eternal.

The self that despairs will undoubtedly experience it as negative. Even so, Kierkegaard thinks despair serves a purpose in the development of a self. Anti-Climacus says: "Consequently it is an infinite merit to be able to despair. And yet not only is it the greatest misfortune and misery actually to be in despair."[17]

Despair is a sickness of the spirit. The sickness of despair is rooted in the very structure of the self. It is, says Anti-Climacus, "the possibility of this sickness [that] is man's advantage over the beast."[18] Despair is not an imbalance within the structure of the self; rather, it is an imbalance in the relation (by which we relate to ourselves). We are not always mis-relating to ourselves. Rather, despair represents a certain fall from grace. Anti-Climacus remarks, "Nor could he despair unless the synthesis were originally in the right relationship to the hand of God."[19] We were in the correct relation to ourselves, as a Platonic idea of sorts, yet we became mis-related. There is the possibility of going astray, because, as we have already stated, we have freedom. Anti-Climacus says, "... despair is an aspect of spirit, it has to do with the eternal in a person. But the eternal is something he cannot be rid of, not in all eternity. He cannot rid himself of it once and for all; nothing is more impossible."[20] What we are, our pre-given telos, is already determined, and to try to avoid our self is despair.[21]

Death is the cause of the awareness of our sickness. We could readily anticipate the problem a self will encounter, given the understanding of what a self is in Kierkegaard's philosophical theology. Human existence is temporal (unlike concepts); all things come to an end with death. With the end of possibility, it seems that the human situation is bound to lead us into despair.[22]

Anti-Climacus's meditation on despair creates a kind of analytic phenomenology of despair, which can ultimately be reduced to the despair of not wanting to be ourselves. Kierkegaard would have it that despair as such is a universal phenomenon. Anti-Climacus says:

> There is not a single human being who does not despair at least a little, in whose innermost being there does not dwell an uneasiness, an unquiet, a discordance, an anxiety in the face of an unknown something, or a something he doesn't even dare strike up acquaintance with, an anxiety about a possibility in life or an anxiety about himself...[23]

Even in happiness, we can be in despair. Anti-Climacus states that

> deep within good fortune's most hidden recesses, there dwells also the dread that is despair...for that is where despair is most cherished, its choicest dwelling place: deep in the heart of happiness...It is most in dread of nothing.[24]

Happiness is ephemeral and despair has a purpose. It will be through despair that we will come to be ourselves before God. Anti-Climacus thus writes:

> Eternity asks you, and every one of these millions of millions, just one thing: whether you have lived in despair or not, whether so in despair that you did not know that you were in despair, or in such a way that you bore this sickness concealed deep inside you as your gnawing secret, under your heart like the fruit of a sinful love, or in such a way that, a terror to others, you ratted in despair. If then, if you have lived in despair, then

whatever else you won or lost, for you everything is lost, eternity does not acknowledge you, it never knew you, or, still more dreadful, it knows you as you are known, it manacles you to yourself in despair![25]

It is through freedom that we can either perpetuate our *despair of not being who we are*, or become ourselves. "The self is the conscious synthesis of infinitude and finitude, which relates to itself, whose task is to become itself, that can, furthermore, only be done in the relation to God. To become ourselves, however, is to become something concrete."[26] The despair of the eternal is precisely to desire to be boundless when we are in fact shackled to the limits of necessity. Thus: "The self is only healthy and free from despair when, precisely by having despaired, it is grounded transparently in God."[27] Now, we have anticipated Kierkegaard's cure for despair. We can be free from despair (but not free from suffering) by finding our foundation in God. An explication of the God-relationship must be deferred to chapter 3, in order to first further examine the dynamics of the self.

ANALYSIS

When Anti-Climacus began his meditation upon the self, he said that the greatest danger was that of losing the self. With possibility, we can trace one set of ways in which we can lose ourselves. Possibility is a movement away from necessity. One type of despair is focussed upon the possible. We may wish for things that free us from necessity. To wish that we could be free from the very necessities of living is a form of metaphysical rebellion. For example, a person may pay little attention to reality. We can think of the image of "the fool" on tarot cards. This person, usually depicted as a youth, is looking into the distance while walking toward a cliff. The youth is so enchanted by the possibilities of the future that he does not see the necessities; by looking into the distance he misses the very real danger close at hand.

Another type of despair moves in the opposite direction, away from the possible, and hides away in necessity. Anti-Climacus uses a helpful analogy to depict the situation of the self. Necessity is like the parents who give the "okay" to a child's wish, the possible. Some people always think, however, "I cannot do that," because they do not see "that" as a possibility for themselves; they exist within the despair of necessity. The person who denies the possible is prone to melancholy. He is always in fear of danger, thinking of losing security (economic, emotional, and so on) by venturing into the possible (a new job, a new relationship, etc.). Ironically, his melancholic paralysis ensures that he achieves his greatest fear, despair: "He perishes in the dread, or perishes in what it was he was in dread of perishing in."[28] The melancholy person wants to avoid despair of necessity, which may cause losing what is required (e.g., economic security), but dies in despair, albeit a particular variety, the despair of the possible, thinking "nothing is possible." Anti-Climacus writes:

But while one kind of despair steers blindly in the infinite and loses itself, another kind of despair allows itself to be, so to speak, cheated of its self "by others". By seeing the multitude of people around it, by being busied with all sorts of worldly affairs, by being wise to the ways of the world, such a person forgets himself, in a divine sense forgets his own name, dares not believe in himself, finds being himself too risky, finds it much easier and safer to be like the others, become a copy, a number, along with the crowd.[29]

The goal, in the most general and basic sense, is to have some balance between these two facets of the self, necessity and possibility. Anti-Climacus puts the situation well:

> For the purpose of becoming (and the self must become itself freely) possibility and necessity are equally essential. Just as infinitude and finitude belong to the self, so also do possibility and necessity. A self that has no possibility is in despair, and likewise a self that has no necessity.[30]

Just as finitude is the constraining factor in relation to infinitude, Anti-Climacus holds necessity to be the constraining factor for possibility. Whereas the past is a necessity, the future presents itself as a possibility. If someone says "Tell me about yourself," it is no coincidence that you are bound to refer to the past, "I did this, went here, and so forth." Our past is part of ourselves, the people we met, the friends and lovers we had and lost, the joys and traumas: all these things are part of ourselves. Yet, *we are also what we are not yet*, in the sense that we strive into the possible. Anti-Climacus says:

> To the extent that it is itself, it is necessary; and to the extent that it must become itself, it is a possibility. Now if possibility outstrips necessity, the self runs away from itself in possibility so that it has no necessity to return to. This then is possibility's despair...Surely what the self now lacks is actuality; that at least is what would normally be said, and indeed we imply this when we talk of a person's having become unreal. But on closer examination what the self really lacks is necessity.[31]

Actuality, according to Kierkegaard, links the necessary and the possible. At this moment, we are actual and as such are a synthesis of the necessary past and possible future, which reflects back upon itself in self-consciousness.

Kierkegaard's Christian philosophy proposes a remedy, which is necessarily born in the imagination as a possibility: eternal life. Although there is said to be a time, perhaps youth, when we are rich in hope, Anti-Climacus uses hope in two ways. We can distinguish this secular hope from profane hope whose object encompasses all individual things. We are brought into recognizing hope, in the strong sense, when we have hit rock bottom, attained pure despair. According to Kierkegaard, we only experience hope when we are in the depths of despair: only then can hope have any meaning. Anti-Climacus says:

> The decisive moment only comes when man is brought to the utmost extremity, where in human terms there is no possibility. The question is whether he will believe that for God everything is possible, that is, whether he will have faith. But this is simply the formula for losing one's mind; to have faith is precisely to lose one's mind so as to win God.[32]

When all things look like they have come to an end, to believe in possibility is the only way to heal ourselves. As Anti-Climacus puts it:

> Salvation, then, is humanly speaking the most impossible thing of all; but for God everything is possible! This is the struggle of faith, which struggles insanely, if you will, for possibility. For only possibility saves...But for someone who is on the point of despair it is: get me possibility, get me possibility, the only thing that can save me is possibility! A possibility and the despairer breathes again, he revives; for without possibility it is as though a person cannot draw breath.[33]

For example, Kierkegaard's entire meditations upon the stories of Abraham and Job underscore the meaning of faith: believing against all odds. It is for this reason Anti-Climacus says, "to have faith is precisely to lose one's mind." It is by hope that we can believe we can become ourselves, when we are lost. Anti-Climacus again reiterates the centrality of possibility:

> The believer possesses the ever-sure antidote to despair: possibility; since for God everything is possible at every moment. This is the health which resolves contradictions...Health in general is to resolve contradictions...To lack possibility means either that everything has become necessary or that everything has become trivial. The determinist, the fatalist, is in despair, and in despair he has lost his self because everything is necessity...possibility is for the self what oxygen is for the body.[34]

For Kierkegaard, we are both free and determined; possibility coexists with necessity.[35] Finding the right balance requires ethics.

The project of ethics, in fact, remains the same for Kierkegaard as it did for Aristotle, to make *what we now are* into *what we ought to be*. Anti-Climacus likens the becoming of ourselves to coming home.[36] In ancient times, ethics was about how to live so as to fulfill our nature. Kierkegaard is likewise preoccupied with the question, "How should I live my life?"[37]

Many have not been able to fully appreciate Kierkegaard's ethical stance because he has been stereotyped as an existentialist. The English world consumed the post–World War II existentialist movement, after all, largely through the translated writings of Jean-Paul Sartre. Existentialism could be summed up as the following notion: "Man makes himself." Kierkegaard disagrees:

To have individuality is to believe in the individuality of every other person; for individuality is not mine but is God's gift by which He gives me being and gives being to all, gives being to everything. It is simply the inexhaustible swell of goodness in the goodness of God that He, the almighty, nevertheless gives in such a way that the receiver obtains individuality, that He who created out of nothing nevertheless creates individuality so that creation over against him shall not be nothing, although it is taken from nothing and is nothing and yet becomes individuality.[38]

According to Kierkegaard, the origin of the self thus rests in God: the "inexhaustible swell of goodness." He had a traditional scholastic understanding of creation and would have been at odds with Sartre on the issue of whether or not we have a basic nature or are entirely a product of our own creation. The next chapter explicates Kierkegaard's theory of human development.

2

SELF-BECOMING

IN THE PREVIOUS CHAPTER, the self was to some extent described as a fixed structure. However, as the self is always in the process of becoming, development is an essential feature of the self. Kierkegaard's theory of human development comprises three stages: the aesthetic, the ethical, and the religious.

In order to uncover the mechanisms that egg us on from one to the next, we need to review the stages. In this chapter we consider the first two stages of development according to Kierkegaard.

The early stages he describes as being plagued by sin and anxiety. In this chapter, I first consider his notions of sin and anxiety and then examine the aesthetic and ethical stages. The final, religious stage of Kierkegaard's story is discussed in chapter 3.

Sin

According to Anti-Climacus, Socrates equated sin with ignorance. For example, a drunk may think he is living *la dolce vita*. This example is supposed to illustrate that our own perception of our life is not the sole criteria for living the "good life." We could be wrong, that is, in a state of ignorance.[1]

Kierkegaard distinguishes Christian sin from the Socratic conception. Sin, for Kierkegaard, has an ontological place in human existence. He does not shy away from the unpopular idea of "original sin." Kierkegaard holds that this original sin came into the world with sexuality and with women.[2] It was, after all, Eve who is said to have caused the fall of mankind. Christian mythology teaches that it is because of Adam and Eve's actions that we are all born in sin.

Kierkegaard views Adam both as an individual and as an emblem of humanity as a whole: "He [Adam] is himself and the race. Therefore that which explains Adam also explains the race and vice versa."[3] This view has the human race living in the state of sin that was inaugurated by the mythical fall from paradise; this sin is manifested to Kierkegaard in the fact that we have to *become ourselves*. As such, sin serves as the starting point both of the race and of the individual's development. Simply put in the opposite terms: if mankind did not find itself in a state of sin, we would not have to become ourselves but would just be ourselves. Anti-Climacus writes, "Sin is: having been taught by a revelation from God what sin is, before God in despair not to want to be ourselves, or in despair to want to be ourselves."[4]

Anti-Climacus begins his meditation upon the notion of Christian sin by saying that a sin is not just doing wrong but doing it while knowing it to be wrong. There is thus a difference between Socrates' idea of ignorance and the Christian notion. Kierkegaard, for instance, speaks of a "calling," in terms of feeling "called" to be a priest, for example.[5] We have to become ourselves, and can go astray by becoming estranged from our existential calling. Sin results from our not confronting the ensuing sense of despair. However, it should be pointed out that sin cannot be altogether avoided. In fact, according to Kierkegaard, the fleeing from despair is an integral part of the process of becoming ourselves. Anti-Climacus remarks that we can maintain ourselves in sin:

> [I]n the depths to which he has sunk it is his state of sin which holds him together, wickedly strengthening him with its consistency; it is not the particular new sin which—yes, how dreadfully crazy!—"helps" him; the particular new sin is simply their expression of the state of sin, which is really the sin.[6]

Kierkegaard's concept of sin can be manifest in many guises, as evidenced by the various types of despair Kierkegaard catalogues. Sin may even seem to help us live, insofar as it offers a familiar, established way of acting. We may only feel like ourselves in a state of sin, just as the alcoholic does not feel "like himself" when he is sober. Anti-Climacus offers an analysis of how melancholia can be the result of persisting in a sinful state. He writes:

> Sin itself is the struggle of despair, but when energy is exhausted there has to be a new intensification, a new demonic withdrawal into oneself, and that is despair over sin...Through the sin, in other words, through despairing over the sin, he has lost all relation to grace—and also to himself.[7]

For Kierkegaard, sin "concerns every man." Sin is an actuality whereas, to use a point of comparison, logic is not.[8] Kierkegaard remarks, "Sin has its specific place, or more correctly, it has no place, and this is its specific nature."[9] Sin has "no place" because its essential feature is the being out of place, resulting in our not being ourselves. Kierkegaard holds that it is the individual's task to give birth to himself.[10] However, he also notes that "it is the nature of man to go astray one way or another."[11]

ANXIETY

Anxiety is brought into the world with sin. When we despair not being ourselves (or are ourselves in despair), we persist in a state of anxiety. Kierkegaard's use of the term *anxiety* denotes a feeling pertaining to nothing in particular. To compare anxiety to fear: we fear particular things, whereas a state of anxiety does not have or require a specific object. We can just be anxious in general, without being aware of a particular cause of our anxiety. "The object of anxiety is a nothing."[12]

Anxiety is endemic to human existence due to its kinship with freedom and self-consciousness. If we were not conscious, we would not be aware of feelings of anxiety, which demonstrate a reflective attitude of mind. And, interestingly, without freedom there would be no reason to experience anxiety. Kierkegaard puts it thus:

> The actuality of the spirit constantly shows itself as a form that tempts its possibility but disappears as soon as it seeks to grasp for it, and it is a nothing that can only bring anxiety...it is altogether different from fear and similar concepts that refer to something definite, whereas anxiety is freedom's actuality as the possibility of possibility.[13]

Anxiety "is neither a category of necessity nor a category of freedom; it is entangled freedom, where freedom is not free in itself but entangled, not as necessity, but in itself."[14] The root of anxiety is not freedom constrained by circumstance but, rather, the intrinsic constraint of freedom itself. It is as if we have arrived at a type of paralysis through being confronted with possibility.

Being confronted with freedom can be a vertiginous experience, which leads to anxiety. "Hence anxiety is the dizziness of freedom, which emerges, looks down into its own possibility, laying hold of finiteness to support itself. Freedom succumbs in this dizziness."[15] When we find ourselves lost, estranged from ourselves, there will inevitably be anxiety, as almost anything is possible.

Kierkegaard distinguishes between subjective and objective anxiety. Subjective anxiety refers to the inauguration of sin in the individual, whereas objective anxiety refers to the fact that sin came into the world with the very first chapter of the human race. Objective anxiety refers to a fact about human nature, whereas its subjective counterpart is its manifestation in an individual. "Subjective anxiety is the anxiety that is posited in the individual and is the consequence of his sin...By coming into the world sin acquired significance for the whole creation. This effect of sin in nonhuman existence I have called objective anxiety."[16]

Anxiety is essentially rooted in a certain relation to time. Kierkegaard refers to temporal time and the eternal. The former is always in a state of flux, while the latter is constant. At one point it seems that Kierkegaard comes close to collapsing the eternal within the temporal world:

> The present, however, is not a concept of time, except precisely as something infinitely content less, which again is the infinite vanishing...The eternal, on the contrary, is the present...The present is the eternal, or rather, the eternal is the present, and the present is full...[If] time and eternity touch each other, then it must be in time, and now we have come to the moment...A blink is therefore a designation of time, but mark well, of time in the fateful conflict when it is touched by eternity.[17]

For the intellect, according to Hegelian Platonism, the moment is eternal; it is constantly passing away and being replaced. Yet, in Kierkegaard's nominalism, the eternal is always in a real conflict with the moment, because the moment is fleeting, whereas the eternal is constant.

In fact, "If a human being were a beast or an angel, he could not be in anxiety. Because he is a synthesis, he can be in anxiety...Anxiety is freedom's possibility, and only such anxiety is through faith absolutely educative, because it consumes all finite ends and discovers all their deceptiveness."[18] As he points out, if we were beasts or angels, there would be no freedom, no sin, no anxiety, and, hence, no need of salvation. The salvation to which we refer and aspire requires recognition of the "deceptiveness" of the finite. "Now the anxiety of possibility holds him prey until, saved, it must hand him over to faith."[19]

Insofar as sin is to be conquered, anxiety is to be overcome. Kierkegaard writes: "Only in the moment that salvation is actually posited is this anxiety overcome...When salvation is posited, anxiety, together with possibility is left behind."[20] Kierkegaard is quick to point out that anxiety is never annihilated but comes to play another role after salvation. If we are constantly striving to be ourselves, we are in a state of longing; but when we can reside in ourselves fully, only then, he contends, do we achieve freedom from anxiety.

A CURE

Becoming ourselves will require, according to Kierkegaard, establishing a firm belief in God. The main point in establishing a relationship to truth is not that we have to travel here or there to discover it. Kierkegaard says, "Life is rich enough, if only one understands how to see. One need not travel to Paris and London; besides, this would be of no help if we are unable to see."[21]

If we picture the individual floating along, as it were, through the continuity of time, which forms his past, while orienting him toward the future, we can conceive of a break in this continuity. The break is called "the sudden." The sudden is a disruption in the continuity of the self. We become estranged from ourselves, and the effect of this alienation is inclosing reserve. As Kierkegaard puts it:

> The sudden is a new expression for another aspect of inclosing reserve...[which] is the effect of the negative self-relation in the individuality. Inclosing reserve closes itself off more and more from communication. But communication is in turn the expression for continuity, and the negation of continuity is the sudden.[22]

The sudden is anxiety about the good, which Kierkegaard terms "the demonic." "The good signifies continuity, as the first expression of salvation is continuity...The sudden is always due to anxiety about the good."[23] The break in the continuity of the self is always due to a concern over truth, or the eternal. When there is a break within the continuity of the self, there is an inclosing reserve which is a withdrawal. The sudden breaks our relation with ourselves. "The sudden is a complete abstraction from continuity, from the past and from the future."[24] The inclosing reserve, as the effect of this break, brings the self in upon itself (as a withdrawal from the correct way of being ourselves).

The cure for the ailments of the self, or in positive terms the fulfilment of what it is to be a self, comes with the acquisition of truth. "Viewed intellectually, the content of freedom is truth, and truth makes man free. For this reason, truth is the work of freedom, and in such a way that freedom constantly brings forth truth."[25] For Kierkegaard, freedom is opposed to the sudden. He holds that truth makes man free. Yet, what we need to understand is what Kierkegaard means by the word "truth". He does not think that mere facts (truth) set one free. For example, it is "true" that, given certain purities of water and atmospheric pressures, water will boil at one hundred degrees Celsius. Of course, Kierkegaard does not think the realization of this fact or truth will make one free. Rather, truth is something to be attained, actualized, lived. In short, truth is not some objective fact that we can look at disinterestedly, as a spectator in a laboratory. If we mobilize our freedom toward this end, toward self-becoming, we will be using our freedom to bring forth truth. Kierkegaard writes that

> truth is for the particular individual only as he himself produces it in action. If the truth is for the individual in any other way, or if he prevents the truth from being for him in that way, we have a phenomenon of the demonic...[26]

Kierkegaard notes that truth has always had its "loud proclaimers" and there has been much talk in modern times of truth, but he is interested in whether we will let truth "permeate [our] whole being," and "vindicate certitude and inwardness...in an entirely concrete sense."[27] Truth has to be something of great subjective, passionate importance to the individual; it has to be a matter of "inwardness...in an entirely concrete sense." As Kierkegaard says, "Inwardness is an understanding, but in concreto..."[28]

Kierkegaard has said that the realization of truth for the individual requires freedom and action. To understand how these terms relate to inwardness, we can consider this passage:

> The most concrete content that consciousness can have is consciousness of itself, of the individual himself—not the pure self-consciousness, but the self-consciousness that is so concrete that no author, not even the one with the greatest power of description, has ever been able to describe a single such self-consciousness, although every single human being is such a one...This self-consciousness, therefore, is action, and this action is in turn inwardness, and whenever inwardness does not correspond to this consciousness, there is a form of the demonic as soon as the absence of inwardness expresses itself as anxiety about its acquisition.[29]

Every individual who is conscious of himself is conscious in a very intimate way that never admits full explication. Consciousness reflecting upon itself is an "action." It is this action that Kierkegaard deems "inwardness." When he wants us to relate to truth subjectively, he hopes we will orient ourselves towards the truth by turning inward, toward ourselves. To be self-conscious does not imply contemplation or reflection per se, as if to suggest we can think about ourselves as an object. There is a deeper core to the self, which is self-conscious in such a way that we are not alienated from ourselves. It is in fact reflection that leads to the lack of inwardness.[30]

Kierkegaard defines inwardness in terms of earnestness:

> I am not aware that there exits a single definition of earnestness...but because in relation to existential concepts it always indicates a greater discretion to abstain from definitions, because a person can hardly be inclined to apprehend essentially in the form of definition what must be understood differently, what he himself has understood in an entirely different way, and which in the form of definition easily becomes something else, something foreign to him. Whoever loves can hardly find joy and satisfaction, not to mention growth, in preoccupation with a definition of what love properly is.[31]

With concepts that are related to human existence, such as the "self," we can never fully define them as we can a triangle (that thing which has three sides, etc.).

Having cautioned our enthusiasm for definitions and explanations, we can now cautiously proceed to consider what Kierkegaard means by "earnestness," since he equates it with inwardness. Kierkegaard does not use the term *earnest* to refer to being earnest about this or that thing. There is only one object for earnestness. "This object every human being has, because it is himself."[32] Further, Kierkegaard states: "Inwardness, certitude, is earnestness...Inwardness is therefore eternity or the constituent of the eternal in man."[33] Basically, inwardness indicates a sort of communion with one's self.

We shall now begin moving beyond the scaffolding of human development, which takes on dialectical form:

(1) problem (sin/despair)
(2) recognition of sin (anxiety)
(3) cure (salvation/becoming ourselves)

We shall turn to the first stage of human development according to Kierkegaard, the aesthetic, where the holy trinity of sin, despair, and anxiety find their unique form of expression.

THE AESTHETIC STAGE

The essential characteristic of the aesthetic stage is temporality, whose flower is pleasure. It is not entirely surprising then that Kierkegaard uses "women" to symbolize the aesthetic stage of existence. The aesthete is a "seducer" of women. Kierkegaard contrasts the man of ideas to those who "hanker after a skirt." Whereas ideas are eternal, women represent the temporal world of pleasure in Kierkegaard's philosophy. He writes:

> A woman comprehends the finite; she understands it from the ground up...the finite can presumably make a person happy, infinite per se never... Woman explains the finite; man pursues the infinite...woman bears children in pain, but man conceives ideas in pain...But because woman explains the finite in this way, she is man's deepest life, but a life that is supposed to be hidden and secret, as the life of the root always is.[34]

Kierkegaard also says of women: "[S]he is the immediacy. Only in this immediacy is she a goal for his desire, and therefore I said that he desires immediacy not spiritually but sensually."[35] Similarly, pleasure focuses us upon the moment, it does not dwell on the past or future. For Kierkegaard, women represent the aesthete's desire: the constant seeking of pleasure.

Language is a medium that negates the sensuous.[36] Language entails reflection and thus moves us away from the "now". Language is thought. Whereas language annuls the immediate, music, by refection, lives in the immediate. The ideal of the poet-existence is music, in that it exists in the same categories as the sensuous-erotic, immediacy.[37] The essential aesthete is one who lives the poet-existence. Kierkegaard writes, "What is a poet? An unhappy person who conceals profound anguish in his heart but whose lips are so formed that as sighs and cries pass over them they sound like beautiful music."[38] Generally speaking, the aesthetic mode of existence is linked, in many of Kierkegaard's examples, to youth, a time when we are generically assumed to be preoccupied with the pleasures of the temporal world.

Kierkegaard's cursory remarks on mysticism crystallize in the complaint that the mystic tries to exist by mood and makes the mistake of choosing metaphysical, and not ethical, repentance.[39] The mystic denies the world as an illusion, and hence cannot maintain an ethic. Kierkegaard paints the mystic much like the poet, as someone with a hankering for the moment of rapture.

It is not surprising that Kierkegaard values language over music. Although he recognizes that music intoxicates us in the ecstasy of the moment, he does not see it as providing a lasting cure to anxiety. Music may free us from anxiety by immersing us in the present, but it does not do this permanently.[40]

In fact, according to Kierkegaard, when people are born, there are two classes, the masses (others) and individuals (the nobility). Kierkegaard says that when God created Adam and Eve, he created others (the masses) to cure boredom. (In fact, he thinks it is out of boredom that man entertains himself by trying to build the tallest tower, which only becomes a testimony to his boredom.) The sensualist is always trying to achieve pleasure, which means, de facto, avoiding boredom.[41]

The aesthetic stage of development is represented in Kierkegaard's edifice by the seducer. The aesthetic existence is, ultimately, an unhappy existence in that it is never satisfied. The "unhappy one" is the person who locates his essential nature outside himself.[42] Yet, in the end, the aesthete is absent from himself by being lost in the past (recollection) or future (hope). Either he recollects past pleasures (the old man), or hopes for future ones (the seducer), but can never reside in the present—and therefore in the forever. Either way, there is an imbalance within the self. Recognition of our sickness is experienced as a blow. The mistake of the seducer, or poet-existence, the Don Juan, is to try to exist in the moment alone.

When we discover the ephemeral nature of such an existence, we are confronted by the emptiness left us by fleeting pleasures. It is significant that the epigram for *Either/Or I*, reads: "Greatness, knowledge, renown, Friendship, pleasure and possessions, All is only wind, only smoke: To say it better, all is nothing." Indeed, given the ephemeral nature of the world and all its voluptuous pleasures, it could be likened to smoke. The world has no substance for Kierkegaard as it is not permanent. Thus, Kierkegaard will speak of "the glittering bondage of pleasure,"[43] "desires shameful fraud,"[44] and being "ensnared by the world."[45] Kierkegaard is convinced that the temporal world can never provide fulfilment, only ephemeral happiness, and this leads him to take flight from the world. The world is something that offers all sorts of enticing pleasures, yet these are "frauds" that "ensnare" us, in that they lead only to despair, and to stay in such a state is a sin, which in turn results in anxiety. The theme of abandonment, resignation, and flight from the world is ubiquitous in Kierkegaard's thought. His own personal break with Regine Olsen becomes a necessary step in the flight from the world to a more secure foundation.

It is noteworthy that Kierkegaard's orientation toward the world exemplifies several passages from the New Testament. For instance, in Romans we read, "For the mind set on the flesh is death, but the mind set on the spirit is life and peace."[46] In the Psalms it is written, "Man is like mere breath; His days are like passing shadows…Surely every man at his best is a mere breath. Surely every man walks about as a phantom."[47] According to Kierkegaard, the first step towards building a coherent self is to progress from the aesthetic to the ethical.

THE ETHICAL STAGE

Whereas the aesthete attempts to live solely in the here and now, the "ethical" individual goes beyond the immediacy by a commitment to duty.[48] Kierkegaard admits that the seducer's diary was to mark the move to the ethical, which is lasting. When we commit to something, such as duty, we are bound to something beyond the present. The prototype of duty is marriage. In marriage, we are committed to something that requires us to act not on how we feel in this or that moment but in relation to a duty. "The person who lives aesthetically…is always living in the moment…in the ethical I am raised above the moment, I am in freedom."[49] In the ethical mode of existence we are still actualizing our commitment to duty in the present. Yet, what is guiding our actions this moment is an idea, like marriage, which goes beyond the now.

Kierkegaard uses many analogies from human existence to depict his conception of human development. He uses the vivid image of the "first love" to represent the aesthetic stage of existence. It is not that the aesthetic is eclipsed by the ethical, but transfigured rather. The aesthete's love is preserved in the ethical, manifest as commitment and duty.[50]

The movement from the aesthetic existence to a moral one requires a "determination of will." An aesthetic life will sooner or later force us, through despair, to seek an alternative. In order to escape the despair of constant craving, we commit our self to an ethical mode of existence. The ethical and ensuing stages are the fulfilment of an inner teleology of the self, where there is a sublimation of the intentions of the previous stage. For example, the duty involved in marriage, claims Kierkegaard, allows us to love fully, which ironically was precisely the aesthetic goal. As Kierkegaard puts it:

> If this [duty] does not already exist in embryo in the first love, then its appearance is naturally very disturbing. But such is not the case with marital love, which in the ethical and the religious already has duty within itself, and when duty manifests itself to them it is not a stranger, a shameless outsider...No, he comes as an old intimate, as a friend, as a confidant whom the lovers both know in the deep secrecy of their love.[51]

At times, Kierkegaard views the self as a house, wherein the basement is the "low" place where the erotic dwells, and the "high" place is where the intellect dwells.[52] In the aesthetic mode of being we live by mood. Yet, in the ethical stage of development, mood is a characteristic or attribute of the self (but not co-extensive with the self). The world exists for humans, according to Kierkegaard, by the grace of God.[53] It is the ethical that works toward our fulfilment.[54] He says, "The individual has his teleology within himself, has inner teleology, is himself his teleology; his self is the goal toward which he strives."[55]

Duty, thus, does not just range over relations to others. Our own work, for instance, is duty. As Kierkegaard writes, "In respiration the organism enjoys its freedom, and thus I, too, have enjoyed my freedom in this writing, the freedom that is mine everyday."[56] Kierkegaard speaks at length of finding one's vocation in life; he terms it one's "calling."[57] As he also writes, "The duty to work in order to live, expresses the universally human, and in another sense expresses the universal also for it expresses freedom."[58] Kierkegaard's concept of duty, one may wish to notice, does not just apply to others in what has become the typical modern (Christian) conception of ethics, which Kierkegaard would call civil morality.[59] Neither, however, is duty understood in the ancient sense of attaining virtue, as perfecting ourselves. Both views complement each other.

Kierkegaard was frustrated with the philosophies of his own day, which seemed to try to explain the entire world yet offer no advice for the individual. The metaphysicians of Kierkegaard's day (e.g., Hegel), are on Kierkegaard's reading submerged in necessity, fatalism, the logic of history, and so on, and thus divorce themselves from possibility. Without possibility there would be no question of ethics, because there would be no freedom.

The negative expression of freedom, according to Kierkegaard, is suicide. Here, we are obviously using our freedom, yet we are using it in a revolt against ourselves. It would seem that suicide would be the most natural expression of asceticism. Yet, Kierkegaard does not suggest we kill ourselves, and this is significant. We are asked, rather, to live in the world, ethically, and this task, he tells us, is the actualization of truth. To actualize truth is to come back to what we are. As Heraclitus had put it, "The soul has a *logos* which increases itself."[60] Yet why cannot self-becoming terminate at the ethical stage? I turn to this question in the next chapter.

3

THE GOD-RELATIONSHIP

I SHALL ATTEMPT TO EXPLAIN WHY, according to Kierkegaard, we have to adopt the religious mode of existence in order to find fulfilment. We need to understand why self-development cannot come to fruition at the ethical stage. In this chapter, we will see that for Kierkegaard a relationship to God is the only secure foundation of ethics. I begin with a description of the religious stage.

THE RELIGIOUS STAGE

The biblical story of Abraham depicts the ordeal of having to throw into question the ethical for the religious. Abraham is asked to kill his son, and has to will himself to believe in the face of uncertainty. As Kierkegaard writes, "He destroys his happiness in the world in order to have his happiness with God—and now if he has misunderstood God—where shall he turn?"[1]

The main theme in these stories is loss and recovery. The religious stage recovers, in fact, redoubles, what has been lost. In Kierkegaard's thought experiments, we have seen what it means to live by pleasure and commitment. Yet, there is an emptiness that haunts us—the loss—and fulfilment is what is hoped to be recovered in the religious stage, the redoubling. Johannes de Silentio, the pseudonym used to write *Fear and Trembling*, provides us with the following example of Kierkegaard's religious writings:

> When the child has grown big and is to be weaned, the mother virginally conceals her breast, and then the child no longer has a mother. How fortunate the child who has not lost his mother in some other way!... When the child is to be weaned, the mother, too, is not without sorrow, because she and the child are more and more to be separated, because the child who first lay under her heart and later rested upon her breast will never again be so close. So they grieve together the brief sorrow. How fortunate the one who kept the child so close and did not need to grieve any more![2]

Kierkegaard writes, however, "Separation forced its way in everywhere to bring pain and unrest, but there is rest!"[3] The rest is gained through a special relationship to knowledge, which Kierkegaard calls "faith." Johannes de

Silentio remarks, "But Abraham had faith, and therefore he was young, for he who always hopes for the best grows old and is deceived by life, and he who is always prepared for the worst grows old prematurely, but he who has faith—he preserves the eternal youth."[4] For Kierkegaard, faith yields belonging.

According to Johannes de Silentio some types of knowledge are yielded by human reason, but faith is the best response to that which is absurd. Johannes sees (instrumental) reason as that which will deny metaphysical truth, "in worldly shrewdness, in petty calculation, in paltriness and meanness, in everything that can make man's divine origin doubtful."[5] Given the despair experienced during our self-becoming, we do indeed have little reason to believe we have a relationship to a benevolent God. Yet, he writes, "The deeper natures never forget themselves and never become anything other than what they were."[6]

The religious stage does not annul the ethical mode of existence but transfigures it. The ethical took the love of the aesthete and perfected it in marriage. So the process goes on. Johannes de Silentio says:

> His love for that princess would become for him the expression of an eternal love, would assume a religious character, would be transfigured into a love of the eternal being, which true enough denied the fulfilment but nevertheless did reconcile him once more in the eternal consciousness of its validity in an eternal form that no actuality can take away from him.[7]

The aesthetic experience of love becomes a commitment, which is then abstracted from the world unto the "eternal being." Love is retained yet again transfigured.

The way to achieve a relation to truth qua truth, and fulfil ourselves, is through faith. At times faith is characterized as the paradox that the single individual is higher than the universal, that is, the ethical.[8] For example, in the story of Abraham there is what Kierkegaard calls a teleological suspension of the ethical. Put simply, we have to suspend the ethical (Abraham has to kill his son) for God. The point is not a literal one, in that we have to be unethical to achieve the religious. The moral of the story is twofold. There is the incipient idea of sacrificing worldly things—a son—for something above the world. But more crucially, the story of Abraham is a lesson in faith.

When Abraham is asked to sacrifice his son, he is asked to do something absurd. To have faith then is to act in the midst of the absurd. To believe that life makes sense is to have faith when, perhaps, there does not seem any good reason for doing so. "God is a friend of order,"[9] as Anti-Climacus says. Faith is termed by Kierkegaard as a passion that allows us to place ourselves "in absolute relation to the absolute."[10]

Faith affirms the inner will over the outer circumstances. As in the case of Abraham, the outer circumstances seemed absurd. Johannes de Silentio writes: "But faith is the paradox that interiority is higher than exteriority."[11] Faith has more to do with perception than with any actual state of affairs. If we view the same situation through faith it appears in a different light than if we do not. Thus, when the exterior world seems impossible, faith changes this perception by affirming the interior will or vision over the exterior circumstance.

Also, there is a change in our relationship to time. Kierkegaard remarks, "There is still one thing of which the simplest and most profound person must, if he talks about it, talk mysteriously—that is: time."[12] We may wish to recall that the aesthete exists by the moment alone. At the aesthetic stage we could be said to be egoistic. Conversely, the ethical person is committed to what goes beyond the here and now. With the ethical there is the commitment to others. The religious brings us back to the moment when we have to take a leap of faith. In *Philosophical Fragments*, Johannes Climacus, another pseudonym, engages the philosophical tradition more than in any other of Kierkegaard's works. He writes of the moment at length:

> If the moment is posited, the paradox is there, for in its most abbreviated form the paradox can be called the moment. Through the moment, the learner becomes untruth; the person who knew himself becomes confused about himself and instead of self-knowledge he acquires the consciousness of sin etc., for just as soon as we assume the moment, everything goes by itself…all offence is in its essence a misunderstanding of the moment, since it is indeed offence at the paradox, and the paradox is the moment.[13]

Johannes Climacus writes, "But such a being that nevertheless is a non-being is possibility, and a being that is being is indeed actual being or actuality, and the change of coming into existence is the transition from possibility to actuality."[14] What becomes actual with regards to our selves, occurs in freedom, and can be traced back to free choice. "All coming into existence is actuality; the transition takes place in freedom. No coming into existence is necessity…"[15] We return to the moment in the religious by making a choice in the now.

Furthermore, in the religious, we also return to the egotistical. As Johannes de Silentio remarks:

> The knight of faith has simply and solely himself, and therein lies the dreadfulness[16]…the knight of faith, who in the loneliness of the universe never hears another human voice but walks alone with his dreadful responsibility. The knight of faith is assigned solely to himself; he feels the pain of being unable to make himself understandable to others…[17]

One thing that is brought out in the story of Job more clearly perhaps is the consequence of faith, which Kierkegaard terms "repetition."[18] For the Greeks, truth was a matter of recollection, remembering something forgotten. Whereas recollection moves backwards, repetition moves forward. Constantin Constantius, the pseudonym used to write another of Kierkegaard's religious works, *Repetition*, writes:

> He alone is truly happy who is not deluded into thinking that the repetition should be something new, for then one grows weary of it... He who wills repetition is a man, and the more emphatically he is able to realize it, the more profound a human being he is. But he who does not grasp that life is a repetition and that this is the beauty of life has pronounced his own verdict and deserves nothing better than what will happen to him anyway—he will perish...it will be manifest whether one has the courage to understand that life is a repetition and has the desire to rejoice in it.[19]

This brings to mind process ontologies, where there is talk of the constant repetition of day and night, summer and winter, and so on.[20] At one point, Constantin Constantius goes as far as to speak of repetition in metaphysical terms: "If God himself had not willed repetition, the world would not have come into being...the world continues, and it continues because it is in repetition."[21] Repetition is also linked to actuality, and the person who wills it is said to be "mature in earnestness." At one point, repetition is referred to as "transcendence."[22] It is fair to say, I think, that Kierkegaard uses the word *repetition* in more than one way; the important thing is to identify the canonical meaning.

We can move from seeing repetition metaphysically, as a feature of the world itself, to viewing it ethically, as a description of human development. As a rule, however, repetition is a category applicable to human beings.[23] Repetition is deemed a task for freedom, which, in Kierkegaard's terms, only humans posses.[24] Repetition lies in recovering ourselves. This recovery of ourselves occurs at the religious stage. Hence, Kierkegaard writes, "Repetition progresses along this path until it signifies atonement, which is the most profound expression of repetition."[25]

The story of Job serves to illuminate human development, and as such to illustrate repetition. To recall the story, Job has everything taken away from him by God. Job is made to suffer. "This category, ordeal, is not aesthetic, ethical, or dogmatic—it is altogether transcendent."[26] Thus Kierkegaard says, "'Repetition' remains a religious category...Eternity is indeed the true repetition in which history comes to an end and all things are explained."[27]

The story of Job is a metaphor for human development: innocence put to an ordeal. The regaining of what was lost, ourselves, signifies a repetition. Job does not just get back what was taken from him, he gets it back doubled. Similarly, Kierkegaard wants to maintain that when we leave the aesthetic life, we get everything back doubled. In short, the salvation of faith gives us more than we could ever hope for as aesthetes.

Constantin Constanius writes: "A poet's life begins in conflict with all life. The point is to find reassurance, for he must always lose the first conflict, and if he wants to win immediately, then he is unjustified."[28] The final stage is the religious when we gain a special relationship to knowledge. Under a pseudonym, Kierkegaard writes of the result of faith:

I am myself again. This "self" that someone else would not pick up off the street I have once again. The split that was in my being is healed; I am unified again. The anxieties of sympathy that were sustained and nourished by my pride are no longer there to disintegrate and disrupt. Is there not, then, a repetition? Did I not get everything double?[29]

The term we can use is "redoubling."

Hitherto, we have spoken of terms such as "the sudden," "despair," "anxiety," and so on. These terms all suggest an ordeal, a break in continuity. In terms of development, we could envision a person who lives for momentary pleasure or relief, such as a drug addict (the ideal Freudian child), who at a certain point reaches such despair as to cause a break of some kind in this mode of existing. As we find written in the Psalms, "But God will break you down forever; He will snatch you up, and tear you away from your tent, And uproot you from the land of the living."[30]

According to Kierkegaard, it is when we have reached the rock bottom depths of our being that we undergo the critical ordeal. "Here only repetition of the spirit is possible, even though it is never so perfect in time as in eternity, which is the true repetition...I am born to myself...the one who is in labour cannot give birth." We are born, and *then* we have to become ourselves. By saying we have *become ourselves*, Kierkegaard wants to indicate the fruition of the teleology of the spirit. Kierkegaard's poetical treatment of human development is celebrated in these words:

> Three cheers for the flight of thought, three cheers for the perils of life in service to the idea, three cheers for the hardships of battle, three cheers for the festive jubilation of victory, three cheers for the dance in the vortex of the infinite, three cheers for the cresting waves that hide me in the abyss, three cheers for the cresting waves that fling me above the stars![31]

The ordeal we have to go through to become ourselves could be understood as the hardships of battle. Human beings do not just require knowledge about this or that specific thing, but also a general understanding that sets in context all other activities we do; Kierkegaard thinks the only way to render the world truly intelligible is through faith. The entire movement is towards abstraction from the finite to the infinite. More specifically, there is a "God-relationship."[32] In the religious mode of existing, we attain a relationship to God by faith.

MOTIVATION

According to Kierkegaard, the ethical mode of existence cannot put an end to despair. The religious mode of existing is the fulfilment of the human being. Kierkegaard writes, "There is a power in a human being that can defy the whole world."[33] The power referred to is the eternal. He remarks:

> Or can you think of anything more appalling than having it all end with the disintegration of your essence into a multiplicity, so that you actually became several, just as the unhappy demonic became a legion, and thus

you would have lost what is the most inward and holy in a human being, the binding power of the personality?[34]

The disintegration of self is one effect of a misrelation to ourselves, which may lead to various types of mental illness. For instance, in his own words, Kierkegaard calls depression a hysteria of the spirit.[35] Also, he offers a cursory analysis of insanity: "There is an absolute misrelation between what the understanding is capable of doing and the task enjoined. The insanity manifests this misrelation."[36]

Kierkegaard says that if there is one wish we could make for another it would be to enjoy freedom from confusion.[37] A parable used by Kierkegaard is that of a sailor who is on a changing sea, but looks to the unchanging sky.[38] The sea is like the world, and we need something permanent—eternal—by which to fix our changing place. Kierkegaard says, "Time can neither substantiate nor refute it, because faith expects an eternity"[39] and "My expectancy was not in the world but in God."[40] The desire to achieve a relationship with God is juxtaposed to "the world."[41] Yet, he says, "The goal is God, and in this sense patience teaches trust in life, and probably its purpose is poor in attire, but inwardly it is glorious, faithful, and unswerving at all times."[42] By enjoying a relation to God we are given that very faith in life that allows us to live.

Faith is motivated by suffering. Kierkegaard urges those who feel despair to take solace in the story of Job, a narrative of one who overcame despair. Kierkegaard writes:

> Job faithfully accompanies him [the person in despair] and comforts him, not, to be sure, as if he had suffered once and for all what would never be suffered again, but comforts as someone who witnesses that the horror has been suffered, the horror has been experienced, the battle of despair has been fought to the glory of God, for his own rescue, for the benefit and joy of others.[43]

"Earthly craving" has to be abandoned, on Kierkegaard's model of development, to make way for the religious. The soul, however, is a contradiction, being composed of the temporal and eternal. (He claims that if there was no contradiction in the soul, we could live in harmony with the moment since, presumably, we would not need to strive for permanence.)[44]

Since the self orients itself toward the future, possibility, this always leaves room for uncertainty. "Not only did he lose himself who danced the dance of pleasure until the end, but also the one who slaved in worry's deliberations and in despair wrung his hands night and day."[45] So it is not only by remaining in the aesthetic mode of existing that we can never become ourselves, but we equally thwart ourselves by endless wallowing in despair.

If we live in anxiety over the past or future, we will be absent from the present. Health, as the cliché goes, lies in being able to dwell in the present. To dwell in the present is not to give way to a poet-existence, because even the ethical has to affirm its commitment to duty in the moment. (The ethical ideal must be actualized in the present.) Similarly, the religious stage requires patience to deal with the present. "Patience has discovered the danger and the terror, but it also comforts: Today we shall do this, tomorrow that, God willing...And yet the purpose is not thereby destroyed; does it not become truly glorious only in this way!"[46] The final goal, becoming ourselves, may seem like an overwhelming task, especially when we are in despair.

Kierkegaard maintains that despair is an error in the will (and thus a sin).[47] Insofar as faith is an act of will, there is some burden put upon the suffering individual to help himself. He states that it is only in trying to be something we are not that we hinder joy.[48] Despair is precisely the resulting condition of not being ourselves. If we were to speak of teleology with respect to the self, we would have to maintain that *what we are* is always in some sense present in the person.

Even though Kierkegaard says "Let youth wear the crown of rosebuds before they wither," he still holds that it is not as if the thought of the eternal is absent from youth. He writes:

> Do not make it prematurely old, lest it drink the bitterness of not being allowed to be young when we are young, and for a second time drink the bitterness of not having been allowed to be young when one was young...thought of the Creator is still youth's most beautiful glory, is also a rosebud, it does not wither.[49]

According to Kierkegaard, when we move from the aesthetic mode of existing to the more developed stages, the temporal "rosebuds" of pleasure wither, but the idea of the eternal remains. Youth is, according to Kierkegaard, the time of life when we experience most of our spiritual growth. In fact, Kierkegaard claims that the thought of truth, first conceived in youth, is what in the end becomes the saving grace of old age.

Kierkegaard's philosophy is permeated with a sense of the importance of the individual will, which is set against losing ourselves in the crowd: non-authenticity. Yet, once we have achieved a God-relationship, through faith, there is recognition. According to Kierkegaard, we realize we are capable of nothing at all. There is surrender to God. "The highest is this: that a person is fully convinced that he himself is capable of nothing at all."[50] Again Kierkegaard says, "Thus man is a helpless creature, because all other understanding that makes him understand that he can help himself is but a misunderstanding, even though in the eyes of the world it is regarded as courageous..."[51] At the height of the religious stage, we are brought to a point of acceptance. Recognizing that we are capable of nothing is co-extensive with acknowledging that God can do everything. By faith in God we are given the power to conquer ourselves, according to Kierkegaard.[52] To conquer ourselves means conquering our desire in the world. The discipline of the self becomes part of our ethical duty.

At the religious stage we come to know ourselves essentially. We do not just know ourselves in relative terms (e.g., by our financial status or attractiveness scale), which always change, but we come to know our essential nature. Kierkegaard introduces the idea of a "first self" by which he wants to indicate the self defined in terms of relations.

> When a person turns and faces himself in order to understand himself, he
> steps, as it were, in the way of the first self, halts that which was turned
> outward in hankering for and seeking after the surrounding world that
> is its object, and summons it back from the external.[53]

Kierkegaard uses the word "hankering" on more than one occasion when
speaking disparagingly of desiring things of the world. The first self is oriented
toward the world; it manifests itself in a "hankering after women," for example.
The essential self knows God through knowing his need for God.[54] The first
self is concerned with the external world, not the internal world.

> Should it have no meaning for him that he is learning ever more and more
> to die to the world, to esteem less and less the external, what life gives and
> takes, what he himself is permitted to achieve in the external world, but
> to be all the more concerned about the internal, about an understanding
> with God...[55]

We have not only the dichotomy that Kierkegaard sets up between temporality
and the eternal but, alongside this, the dualism of the internal and external
world. Kierkegaard writes:

> A person is looking for peace, but there is change: day and night, summer
> and winter, life and death; a person is looking for peace, but there is
> change: fortune and misfortune, joy and sorrow; a person is looking for
> peace and consistency, but there is change...[56]

The theme is recurring: An individual seeks peace from confusion, but he cannot
find it in the external world and hence has to look internally, to God.

When we are oriented toward the world, we live by the values of the world,
and so indulge in pride and cowardliness. Kierkegaard regards pride and
cowardliness as the same thing, in that we are lost to the world of temporality.
In pride we can think that we do not need God, and in cowardliness we can fail
to take a resolution to overcome ourselves. The idea of attaining a reliance on
God is thwarted by pride and cowardliness. It is through faith in God that one
gets the power to conquer oneself (the "first self"). The aesthete has to conquer
himself in order to commit himself to duty, and the religious must have the will
to have faith in order to, paradoxically, surrender before God.

Kierkegaard holds that it is the struggle with truth that gives meaning
to human existence: "But to venture the truth is what gives human life and
the human situation pith and meaning, to venture is the fountainhead of
inspiration, whereas probability is the sworn enemy of enthusiasm..."[57] Truth,
for Kierkegaard, is to have faith in God. When we gain a relation to God through
faith, it is not that God bestows knowledge upon the individual, in the sense of
giving him more facts to carry around with him. Rather, the effect is therapeutic:
we are transfigured by our relation to God. Kierkegaard remarks, "Or was it not

a victory that instead of receiving an explanation from God he was transfigured in God, and his transfiguration is this: to reflect the image of God."[58]

The religious mode of existing, in which we are transformed by faith in God, serves as a remedy to the enigma of being a self. Most notably, according to Kierkegaard, we achieve the fulfilment of self by the religious. The religious stage could be said to be where we achieve what Kierkegaard calls a "purity of heart," which is the will to do and be good. The good is one thing, whereas the world is many things. As a consequence of attaining the religious we are able to overcome ourselves, live in the present, and be free from anxiety and despair. Anxiety persists until the point at which we attain the religious. We may wonder, however, why we should be ethical. If the entire idea is to escape temporality, why not just kill ourselves?

GOD AND ETHICS

I shall in the following draw upon what can be called Kierkegaard's devotional works. Usually, the devotional works are written in the first person (rather than under a pseudonym), since they express Kierkegaard's views directly. (Also, they aspire to reinforce the idea, for the reader, that there is a "total plan" to the edifice.)

Kierkegaard's theory of human development does not, in the end, ask us to abandon the world (and ourselves), as that would not be ethical. At the religious stage, God provides the reason to be ethical. The story of Abraham is a parable, whose lesson is one of faith, and should not be read literally; we should not interpret it as meaning that to be religious one must prepare to be unethical. On the contrary, according to Kierkegaard, the reason we should be ethical is that it is God's will. (God guarantees ethics.) Ethics is the very "home of existence."[59]

Even though Kierkegaard talks about dialectics and repetition, it is not to signify that we are to go through constant changes without end. That is to say, he sees an end to human development, and this end is the religious stage. It is the demonic who, on the other hand, face constant change and never escape repetition.[60]

For illustrative purposes, Kierkegaard constructs imaginary personas that tend toward extremes. Examples of this would be his gender dialectics in which women represent those who live in immediacy, while men represent those who live in the temporal infinity of ideas.[61] Kierkegaard uses womankind to represent the temporal world, and mankind to represent spirit. At times the personages seem close to his own self. It would, in fact, be fair to say that Kierkegaard is more present in his pseudonyms than in the first person narration of his devotional works.

Anyhow, the terror we experience prior to the religious phase is seen as the storm preceding the rainbow, the time when we get everything double. This final end of human development, which accrues in the religious stage, is Kierkegaard's own hope for destination.[62]

Since Kierkegaard's ethics rest on his metaphysics, caring for others does not yield sufficient rewards to make it a good in itself. One way of grasping the relation between the religious and the ethical is by examining Kierkegaard's meditation on "love."

He takes Christian love to be eternal, whereas other types of love, such as the affection between lovers, are seen as transient. "This is precisely its weakness and tragedy, whether it blossoms for an hour or for seventy years—it merely blossoms; but Christian love is eternal."[63] Love between lovers bears the mark of temporality. Like all blossoms it dies. The love that is eternal he deems as Christian.[64] The mark of Christian love, says Kierkegaard, is that it is free of preference. In, what we might call earthly love, love is ruled by preferences. For instance, I like person X, for this or that reason, and do not like person Y for other similarly particular reasons.

Kierkegaard contrasts religious love with ephemeral, worldly love, which he considers a form of self-love. "True love is self-renunciation's love. But what is self-renunciation? It is precisely to give up the present moment and the immediate."[65] Earthly love he takes to be a "rebellion" against what is Christian, insofar as its form of love is based upon inequalities and distinctions. Just as all are made equal in the eyes of God, so too should each be loved equally.

We should have love for others simply because it is through love that we fulfill the law of God, which commands us to love our neighbour. In other words, in being ethical, we are carrying out the will of God. Kierkegaard writes:

> Worldly wisdom thinks that love is a relationship between man and man. Christianity teaches that love is a relationship between: man-God-man, that is, God is the middle term...For to love God is to love oneself in truth; to help another human being is to love God is to love another man; to be helped by another human being to love God is to be loved.[66]

According to Kierkegaard, Christian love requires the "middle term" between man and man. In short, to love God is to love others, the one is manifested in the other: love of God is (supposed to be) evident in the love of others (and ourselves).

Kierkegaard, however, does not posit the human relationship to others as merely some distant effect mediated through our relationship to God. As he says:

> All through the ages everyone who has thought deeply over the nature of man has recognized in him this need for community...the cure is precisely to learn all over again the most important thing, to understand oneself in our longing for community.[67]

These words may surprise the reader of Kierkegaard, in that they see the constant emphasis on individuality and being at odds with society (the public). Even though it is true that one must ultimately stand as an individual (before God), that is, alone, Kierkegaard does not see the need for community as a defect. Rather, he views community as having offered too little for the lonely, and been too much in evidence for those who now seek solitude. The desire for community is an attempt to solve the problem of despair.

Yet, by resting truth on community standards, the spectre of relativism looms large. Kierkegaard states, "But the fact that he really loves the unseen shall be indicated precisely by this, that he loves the brother he sees. The more he loves the unseen, the more he will love the men he sees."[68] The love of God, the unseen, is expressed through ethical actions, which are seen. Kierkegaard warns against loving just the unseen. In other words, Kierkegaard thinks that we should not think we can love God to the exclusion of the world.

To love, says Kierkegaard, is to come into an infinite debt.[69] If we were to think about the idea of a debt, we could see how it gives us a purpose. When we have a debt, we have a task, and this is the ethical. It is worth emphasizing that for Kierkegaard ethics do not just pertain to relations with others, like modern ethics, but also, like ancient ethics, it has to do with ourselves. Hence, Kierkegaard remarks, "To build up by conquering oneself satisfies only love."[70] The task can be seen to have two manifestations: to love others and to conquer ourselves. The relation to ourselves is played out in the ascetic side of Kierkegaard's thought where we have to abandon the temporal world for the eternal.

Kierkegaard asks what good it would be to gain the entire world and yet lose one's soul?[71] The incipient idea is that perhaps there is some conflict between being a person of the world (e.g., in seeking fame and wealth) and the religious quest. Imagination also plays the same role as wishing, emblematized by the gambler. Wishing is temporal and earthly, and thus not aimed at achieving the eternal. Kierkegaard remarks that "earthly hope should be put to death" in order to achieve "true hope."[72] Earthly hope is merely a "wishing" in Kierkegaard's lexicon, whereas hope worthy of the name is aimed at the eternal.

According to Kierkegaard, it is when wishing comes to an end that an experience of the religious can take its beginning. When wishing comes to an end, we enter a "strange land" of loss, as Abraham did when asked to sacrifice his child. A sufferer cannot find solace in the temporal world, so looks to the eternal for a cure.[73] If we are to be crude in order to make the point that Kierkegaard himself arguably makes, we could say that when we fail to find lasting solace in the earthly comforts of, for example, alcohol, women, or money, we start to look away from what laymen call "the world." Kierkegaard openly states, "Commitment to the eternal is the only true salvation." He also uses phrases such as "healed by the eternal," "only the wish pains, while the eternal cures."[74] The eternal could be said to be therapeutic insofar as it "cures" and "comforts." The faculties of imagination or wishing, however, always seek to keep us occupied thinking of new schemes, and thus he pejoratively terms them a cleverness, but nothing more.

Yet Kierkegaard, in Hegelian style, does not wholly eschew any perspective, even the temporal. He acknowledges that we, even when committed to the eternal, are not lifted out of the temporal world. The commitment rather lets us live our earthly life in earnestness, open to being healed by the eternal.[75]

We fulfill our "eternal responsibility" in the ethical by being an authentic individual.[76]

What Kierkegaard calls "the greatest contradiction" is this: "he stands alone—by another's help."[77] The contradiction lies in holding, first, that we stand alone, and second, and at the same time, with another's help. The question that ensues is how we can be alone if we are being helped. The person who helps us in this way is referred to as a "spiritual midwife." The best thing we can do for another, says Kierkegaard, is "to help him stand alone, to become himself, to become his own...inasmuch as it is every human being's essential destiny to become free, independent, to become himself."[78] Similarly, the religious stage puts us in a better and more true relationship to the temporal world through the grace of God. Kierkegaard thinks of suicide, thus, as despair of salvation.[79] And to despair is to abandon or deny God's love.

There is a greater guide in life than imagination (of great import to the aesthete), namely, remorse. Remorse, says Kierkegaard, as well as repentance belong to the eternal in man. Remorse is oriented toward the past, so that we feel bad for this or that thing we have done or omitted doing, and is a call away from evil. Repentance, on the other hand, is aimed at the future, because we can think of the future as the place where we will have the opportunity to repent, and this leads us toward the good. Repentance and remorse are, thus, the two guides on our way to the love of God.[80] In Kierkegaard's own words: "The path is the striving soul's continuant transformation."[81]

One of the more obscure appendages to Kierkegaard's meditation on love is a notion called "like-for-like." Kierkegaard claims that God repeats all that man does and says. Recognizing there are many men doing many different things, it becomes apparent that God's omnipresence and omnipotence allows the like-for-like. "For God is really the pure like-for-like, the pure rendition of how you yourself are."[82] We are never completely alone insofar as God is there, repeating whatever you do. Also, "The word of blessing or judgment which you express concerning someone else, God repeats; he says the same word about you, and this same word is blessing or judgment over you."[83] God commands ethics as his law. According to Kierkegaard, good action brings on further good and bad deeds engender more bad deeds: like-for-like. The like-for-like is like a metaphysical giving and receiving.

With the very trajectory of Kierkegaard's thought toward the eternal, love becomes ontological. It is "the very ground of everything, exists before everything, and remains when everything is abolished."[84] Kierkegaard uses the word "love" as co-extensive with "God" here. Kierkegaard writes, "The only true object of a human being's love is love, which is God, we therefore in a deeper sense are not an object at all, since he is himself love."[85] As Kierkegaard says:

> God is indeed everything, and precisely by having no mine at all self-renunciation's love wins God and wins everything...Only spiritual love has the courage to will to have no mine at all, the courage to abolish completely the distinction between mine and yours, and therefore it wins God—by losing its soul.[86]

By caring about ourselves, we put ourselves into an infinite debt, which means a complete surrendering to God, and an ethical life (through the man-God-man relationship). As is explained in the book of James, "You see that faith was working with [our] works, and as a result of the works, faith was perfected."[87] More precisely, as it says in John, "If we love one another, God abides in us, and His love is perfected in us."[88] According to Kierkegaard, we must embrace the religious stage because it is the only sure foundation for ethics. In the next chapter I delve deeper into what knowledge really means for Kierkegaard.

⌐ 4 ⌐

SELF AND KNOWLEDGE

IN THE PREVIOUS CHAPTER, I explained why, according to Kierkegaard, we have to obtain a relationship to God. I shall now examine the contention that the individual's development reaches its termination in an epistemic situation, that of faith. Yet, I shall attempt to explain how Kierkegaard's claim—that he is the arbiter of truth—does not render truth relative.[1]

The exegetical work done so far requires analysis. We must analyze Kierkegaard's strategy by confronting the tension between his subjectivism and seeming realism. We shall see how Kierkegaard's emphasis upon the subjectivity of truth can be reconciled with his realism, for example, in his belief that there is a God.

MYSELF

Kierkegaard wants to bypass the debate between realism and idealism. He is apt to regard the realist debate as abstract, whereas truth is something we are willing "to live and die" for.[2] Kierkegaard depicts realism in this way:

> There is a truth, the greatness and grandeur of which we are accustomed to praise by saying admiringly that it is indifferent, equally valid, whether anyone accepts it or not; indifferent to the individual's particular condition, whether he is young or old, happy or dejected; indifferent to its relation to him, whether it benefits him or harms him, whether it keeps him from something or assists him to it; equally valid whether he totally subscribes to it or coldly and impassively professes it, whether he gives his life for it or uses it for ill gain...[3]

In his polemic, he perhaps mistakenly assumes that realists are, in their defence of objectivity, personally "unconcerned" about truth. Nonetheless, he does make a point to emphasize the importance of truth to our lives.

He maintains that "objective truths" differ from "concerned truths," which have to be discovered by the individual. (They cannot be passed on as facts in a textbook.) Johannes de Silentio remarks:

> Each generation learns from another, no generation learns the essentially human from a previous one. In this respect, each generation begins

primitively, has no task other than what each previous generation had, nor does it advance further, insofar as the previous generation did not betray the task and deceive themselves.[4]

Some types of knowledge—for example, the truths of mathematics—can be passed down. The task of becoming ourselves, however, requires learning the hard way. Kierkegaard's use of the first person, whether his own or that of his pseudonyms, can be understood as a way "to get men a bit more accustomed to hearing discourse in the first person...to make a turn away from inhuman abstraction to personality—that is my task."[5] Johannes remarks, "I never reason in conclusion to existence, but I reason in conclusion from existence."[6] Johannes Climacus says, "This is quite in order, precisely because decision is rooted in subjectivity, essentially in passion, and maximally in the infinitely interested, personal passion for our eternal happiness."[7]

The extent to which he goes to emphasize subjectivity, however, is equal to the length to which he goes to make it clear he is not pursuing a relativistic line of thought.[8] For instance, he is very critical of the idea that truth may be historical and offers telling words against what today would be called hermeneutics or post-modernism. Anti-Climacus writes:

> Many of the philosophers who were involved in propagating this doctrine of the superiority of the generation over the individual turn away in disgust when **their teaching has sunk to the level where the mob is the God-man. But these philosophers forget that this nevertheless is their teaching, that it was not more true when it was accepted in the best circles, when the elite of the best circles, or a select circle of philosophers, was the incarnation.** [9] [author's own emphasis]

The philosophy of the mob is how Kierkegaard understands relativism. Kierkegaard writes:

> Can a historical point of departure be given for an eternal consciousness; how can such a point of departure be of more than historical interest; can an eternal happiness be built on historical knowledge?[10]

What Kierkegaard craves is an eternal truth on which the self can be based.[11]

Yet, to seek the truth is not to know the object of our inquiry, because if we knew it, we would not be seeking it. Kierkegaard represents truth as being a matter of recollection for the ancients, as if truth was something we have forgotten yet that can be remembered. This is one way in which he can make sense of the claim that truth is a matter of seeking something but we do not know exactly what. Kierkegaard's solution proceeds by trial and error, and terminates with faith. When truth is attained, it causes a transformation, a "conversion," or "new birth."[12]

Kierkegaard is fond of saying that the self is a contradiction (in the specific sense that the structure of the self is composed of opposites). More generally, we can speak of the self as a paradox. Johannes Climacus writes:

> For the paradox is the passion of thought, and the thinker without the paradox is like the lover without passion: a mediocre fellow. This, then, is the ultimate paradox of thought: to want to discover something thought itself cannot think.[13]

Yet, what cannot be thought—let us assume we cannot know God—can be an object of faith. (Of course, we can know the concept, but that does not presuppose empirical interaction.) Kierkegaard paints with a broad brush, calling all knowledge a matter of faith: "Fact is only for faith...The individual is born with faith—that is, with his second nature."[14] Anyhow, since God is paradoxical, it is something we must relate to with faith.

Kierkegaard's views regarding our relation to truth can be drawn out from considering his views on the philosophical enterprise. In *Philosophical Fragments*, Kierkegaard's pseudonym Johannes Climacus seems to be examining Descartes' philosophy, which is known to begin with methodical doubt. Johannes Climacus considers three statements: "(1) philosophy begins with doubt; (2) in order to philosophise, we must have doubted; (3) modern philosophy begins by doubt."[15] Johannes Climacus notes that saying philosophy begins with doubt (the first proposition), is semantically different from saying that doubting is part of philosophy's task after its inception (the second proposition). Furthermore, he notes that although the first two can be taken as universal, the third is an historical point. It is indeed a modern preoccupation with epistemology that sets doubt in the fore, as we see, for instance, in the writings of Descartes.

Also, Johannes Climacus understands there to be three ways in which we can understand the beginning of philosophy: the absolute (e.g., mysticism), the objective (e.g., science), and the subjective beginning (e.g., the existential). For Hegel, according to Kierkegaard, truth was thought to be present as immediate in the absolute beginning of both consciousness and the history of Western philosophy. "The absolute beginning is that concept which is also the end of the system, the concept of absolute spirit."[16] God is everything, including the unfolding of history.

Objective beginning is marked by a deliberative approach to truth. We aim to obtain a generically realist brand of truth. For instance, according to Frege, when we proclaim a mathematical truth it would not matter if the speaker was a madman; the statement would be true or false regardless of the personality of the speaker. In Kierkegaard's polemic, however, a subjective approach to truth makes individual personality a requirement for truth. Since he is not a relativist, however, it would be better to characterize his views as realist, while requiring a certain subjective methodology for its attainment. Johannes Climacus exemplifies the methodology:

> I shall endeavour to think it through to the best of my ability, to do what it says with all my passion, come what may, whether it leads to everything

or to nothing, makes me wise or mad, I shall stake everything but shall not let go of the thought. My visionary dreams about being a follower have vanished; before I was allowed to be young, I became old; Now I am sailing on the open sea.[17]

The sea, in some of Kierkegaard's writings, represents being lost; we are "out at sea." As we may recall, it is to the unchanging sky rather than the heaving waters that Kierkegaard pins his gaze. Johannes has set himself the task of findingout what he can know, and has engaged in doubt. The doubt, as he notes, may lead to wisdom or madness, but he is determined to follow its path. Doubt is not an epistemological problem (how can I know X), but an existential one (how can I live not knowing how). In this regard, Johannes Climacus, more closely than any of the other pseudonyms, seems to be speaking as Kierkegaard himself.

When considering how we should relate to knowledge, Kierkegaard's thought takes its beginning with a negative criticism of how not to relate to truth. Kierkegaard calls Hegel a Johannes Climacus who wants to climb to the heavens with syllogisms. The idea is that we cannot achieve truth by reflection. If we, like Descartes, however, see doubt as central, if not the very origin of philosophy, epistemology gains prominence over ethics. For Kierkegaard, the "I think, therefore I am" should read "I act, therefore I am."

The bottom line for Kierkegaard is that we have to live. In Johannes Climacus, Kierkegaard paints us the picture of a man who feels that he has wasted his life studying philosophy and not arrived at anything in the end but a pit of doubt. Kierkegaard's attitude toward doubt is an elaboration of James's: "[F]or the one who doubts is like the surf of the sea driven and tossed by the wind."[18]

In dealing with doubt, Kierkegaard takes as his point of departure a Hegelian theory of consciousness, which corresponds with the different relationships we can have toward truth and the beginning of philosophy. Each stage, in Hegel's thought, represents a possible way to orient ourselves vis-à-vis the truth. He aims to subsume all the views, the entire history of philosophy, within his own theory. Kierkegaard follows suit thus. The first view:

The beginning of philosophy	Time	Stage
Absolute	Immediacy	Aesthetic

We could begin philosophy with immediacy (the absolute). We could assume philosophy to begin with a relationship to truth. Kierkegaard dismisses stage one as an epistemic and ethical impossibility. Thus, "However much the subject has the infinite within himself, by existing he is in the process of becoming."[19]

The second view:

The beginning of philosophy	Time	Stage
Objectivity	Reflection	Ethical

The objectivity aimed at by science is an example of the second stage. Consciousness, in fact, is taken to be reflective (objective). "Reflection is the possibility of the relation; consciousness is the relation, the first form of which is contradiction."[20] Furthermore, he writes, "Therefore, just as I can say that immediately everything is true, so I can also say that immediately everything is actual, for not until the moment that ideality is brought into relation with reality does possibility appear."[21] Kierkegaard takes language to be a precondition to reflection. "It is language that cancels immediacy; if man could not talk he would remain in the immediate."[22] Words remove us from the immediacy into the notional. The relationship between the ethical and reflection, one may wish to notice, is not exact: according to Kierkegaard, in being concerned with objective truth we may forget "the essential, the innermost, freedom, the ethical."[23] In fact, Kierkegaard says, "Suicide is the only existent consequence of pure thinking."[24] As Johannes Climacus explains, "With respect to existence, thinking is not at all superior to imagination and feeling but is coordinate. In existence, the supremacy of thinking plays havoc."[25] On his analysis, the ancients, for example, wished to exist in the eternal, consequently to do away with the prison of the body.[26] For Greeks (by which he usually means Platonists), "to abandon existence, which continually yields the particular; now there is the opposite difficulty, to attain existence...pure thinking is most distant from existence."[27] Johannes Climacus says of Socrates:

> He was aware that he was a thinking being, but he was also aware that it was existence as medium that perpetually prevented him from thinking in continuity because it continually placed him in a process of becoming. Consequently, in order to be able to truly think, he did away with himself.[28]

Though thought can lead to suicide, nonetheless, there is a generic connection between objectivity and ethics in that reflection is required to will (and hence to be ethical).

Finally, the third view:

The beginning of philosophy	Time	Stage
Subjectivity	Self-consciousness	Religious

In the third stage, philosophy begins with our experiences. Taken collectively, the following story emerges: (1) moment, (2) reflection upon the moment, and (3) the relation to reflection (self-consciousness). When it relates itself to itself, it becomes fully conscious. Johannes Climacus writes:

> Consciousness is mind, and it is remarkable that when one is divided in the world of mind, there are three, never two. Consciousness, therefore, presupposes reflection. If this were not the case, then it would be impossible to explain doubt. Admittedly, language seems to conflict with this, for in most languages, as far as he knew, the term "to doubt"

is etymologically related to the word "two". Yet he surmised that this merely suggested the presupposition of doubt, all the more so since it was clear to him that as soon as mind becomes two, I am *eo ipso* three. If there were nothing but dichotomies, doubt would not exist, for the possibility of doubt resides precisely in the third, which places the two in relation to each other.[29]

The individual is caught between the eternal and the temporal: "Eternity is infinitely quick like that winged steed, temporality is an old nag, and the existing person is the driver..."[30] Johannes Climacus puts it this way: "Human existence has an idea within itself but nevertheless is not an idea-existence...the human being must indeed participate in the idea but is not himself the idea."[31] The idea, like Hegel's absolute, is in motion.

Repetition gives birth to consciousness. "As soon as the question of a repetition arises, the collision is present, for only a repetition of what has been before is conceivable...When ideality and reality touch each other, then repetition occurs. When, for example, I see something in the moment, ideality enters in and will explain that it is a repetition."[32] Kierkegaard writes, "[I]n order to doubt we must will it—the factor of willing must be taken away if we are to stop—consequently we must will to stop it, but then doubt is not at all conquered by knowledge."[33] Doubt is overcome by an act of will, the leap of faith.

For Kierkegaard, unlike Parmenides, for instance, thinking and being are separated by a chasm within existence. "The systematic idea is subject–object, is the unity of thinking and being; existence, on the other hand, is precisely the separation. From this it by no means follows that existence is thoughtless, but existence has spaced and does space subject from object, thought from being."[34] In existence, there is consciousness, which sets itself apart from the world, and as such the world becomes the other. Johannes Climacus writes:

> A system of existence cannot be given...Existence itself is a system—for God, but it cannot be a system for any existing spirit. System and conclusiveness correspond to each other, but existence is the very opposite...Existence is the spacing that holds apart; the systematic is the conclusiveness that combines.[35]

Kierkegaard contends that human beings cannot grasp existence as a system. Our understanding of existence (required to be a full human being) necessitates a submission to God. As Kierkegaard puts things, "It is really the God-relationship that makes a human being a human being, but this is what he would lack,"[36] if faith in God was not established.

GODLESS

I have depicted Kierkegaard's quest as the stages of development in the dialectics of self-becoming. He writes:

A bold venture is not a high-flown phrase, not an exclamatory outburst, but arduous work; a bold venture, no matter how rash, is not a tumultuous proclamation but a quiet dedication that receives nothing in advance but stakes everything.[37]

Abraham can be seen as an example of a character who embarked on a journey and staked everything to reach his destination. Johannes Climacus remarks:

That to finish too quickly is the greatest danger of all. This is a very upbuilding observation that has an extraordinary capacity to stretch out the task, even to the point of going a long way...Generally, speed is lauded and in some instances regarded as neutral, but in this instance it is even reprehensible...So it is also when life is the task. To be finished with life before life is finished with one is not to finish the task at all.[38]

Kierkegaard has remarked that today, not only in the world of business but also in that of ideas, everything is a "real sale": one focuses on the rewards.

Kierkegaard often contrasts authentic existence with the existence of the man on the street (how we should live as opposed to how most people do live). Johannes Climacus remarks, "Or what are those people compared with the god; what is the refreshment of their busy clangour compared with the deliciousness of that solitary wellspring that is in every human being, that well-spring in which god resides, that wellspring in the profound silence when all is quiet!"[39] The ground of the self—God—is ineffable. (Kierkegaard once wrote that humans teach us to speak, but the gods teach us how to be silent.) The individual (set against the community) is the model for authentic existence. Johannes Climacus writes:

An objective uncertainty, held fast through appropriation with the most passionate inwardness, is the truth, the highest truth there is for an existing person...Objectively he then has only uncertainty, but this is precisely what intensifies the infinite passion of inwardness, and truth is precisely the daring venture of choosing the objective uncertainty with the passion of the infinite...Without risk, no faith. Faith is the contradiction between the infinite passion of inwardness and the objective uncertainty...I am "out on 70,000 fathoms of water" and still have faith.[40]

It is through faith in the face of uncertainty that Kierkegaard hopes to achieve the God-relationship "and the corresponding passion of the inwardness of faith."[41]

Johannes Climacus characterizes the great failing of his age as having come to know too much about the world while forgetting inwardness.[42] He speaks of inwardness as the transparency of thought. One difference, for instance, between the aesthetic and ethical stage is the desire to be open in our despair.[43] He explains, "The ethical is the temptation; the relationship with God has come into existence; the immanence of the ethical despair has been broken, the leap has been posited; the absurd is the notification."[44]

Kierkegaard is reacting to an age he viewed as preoccupied with objectivity (in a way that denies subjectivity). Johannes Climacus writes, "I ask for nothing better than to be known in our objective times as the only person who was not capable of being objective."[45] And when not expressing himself through his pseudonyms, Kierkegaard writes in the first person singular.

> If the misfortune of the age is to have forgotten what inwardness is, then one should not write for "paragraph-gobblers", but existing individualities must be portrayed in their agony when existence is confused for them... Therefore if the production is to be meaningful, it must continually have passion.[46]

Kierkegaard maintains that the modern age has forced man to forget how to shape his character (*ethos*) by constantly asking him to look away from himself. Johannes Climacus writes:

> Lest he become important in relation to others, which, far from being inwardness, is external, noisy conduct. If he does that, he will have consolation in the judgement when the god judge that he has made no concessions to himself in order to win anyone...That subjectivity, inwardness, is truth was my thesis.[47]

Johannes Climacus laments, "In Greece a thinker was not a stunted existing person who produced works of art, but he himself was an existing work of art. Surely, to be a thinker should least of all mean to be a variant from being a human being."[48] The effect of being concerned with ourselves is a concern with others. We may wish to recall that, for Kierkegaard, by loving others we love God. Salvation, however, is a purely individual matter; it is the individual who is in despair, and it is he who seeks salvation.

Kierkegaard's salvation also requires an abandonment of temporal pleasure. Johannes Climacus writes: "Eternal happiness is not something higher in rank than a queen [one's beloved] but is the absolute telos...one is better off saying: no, thank you, may I only be allowed to relate myself to the absolute telos."[49] According to Kierkegaard, we are better off with God than with Regina. Yet, Johannes Climacus writes, "The subjective thinker is not a scientist-scholar; he is an artist. To exist is an art. The subjective thinker is aesthetic enough for his life to have aesthetic content, ethical enough to regulate it, dialectical enough in thinking to master it."[50] The religious-minded is able to (and must) dwell in the world (though in an austere manner).

According to Kierkegaard, it is through suffering that the religious relate to eternal happiness. Part of this suffering has to do with being alone, which becomes a virtue. Johannes Climacus writes, "Every human being who has passion is always somewhat solitary; it is only drivellers who are swallowed up in social life."[51] He remarks, "The religious person discovers that what engages him absolutely seems to engage others very little...[he needs] to place a veil between people and himself in order to guard and protect the inwardness of his suffering and his relationship with God."[52]

Furthermore, Kierkegaard thinks that guilt is the greatest expression of existence. Guilt, according to him, expresses our acknowledgement of suffering. The ethical man feels guilt over his life as an aesthete. Guilt also has kinship to the ideas of remorse and repentance. We can have remorse over guilt and seek repentance in the future over it. The ultimate repentance comes, of course, with faith.

Yet, the mechanics of submission are missing from Kierkegaard's discussion of faith. Faith seems to require that one conquer one's will in order to submit oneself to God. Abraham does not just will himself to believe in God's commandments. More precisely, he submits his will to God's. Freedom seems to come from giving it up. In the next chapter, I shall critically reflect upon Kierkegaard's solution by examining his life.

⌐ 5 ⌐

REFLECTIONS AND APPRAISALS

USING BIOGRAPHICAL INFORMATION to assess an argument is regarded as a fallacious line of reasoning, the infamous ad hominem attack. When dealing with the writings of Kierkegaard, however, two reasons allow us to bypass the rule. First, examining Kierkegaard's life can be instructive in understanding his motivations. Second, by Kierkegaard's own standards, his life is relevant. He posits a relationship to knowledge the vital thrust of which emphasizes the relationship between the truths we hold and who we are: "only truth that builds up is the truth for me."[1] Or, as he first said in 1835, his goal was to find the truth that was true for him. What Kierkegaard means can be explained this way. What we consider true can count as so if we can live by it. Also, what we consider true should be yielded by experience: it helps us "build up."

Anti-Climacus says, "The kind of scholarship that is not in the last resort edifying is for that very reason un-Christian. An account of anything Christian must be like a physician's lecture beside the sick-bed."[2] The words of Anti-Climacus are consistent with the connection between our work and life that Kierkegaard authorizes. Just as a doctor deals with the physically sick, the philosopher is to aid one in finding a way to live; that person, first and foremost, is the self. In the previous chapter, I began to critically reflect upon Kierkegaard's theory of the self. We need, however, to be much more aggressive in our criticisms. In this chapter, we shall see how Kierkegaard's life perhaps reflects deficiencies in the socio-historic aspects of his theory of the self. I begin with a look at his life.

LIFE AND PSYCHOLOGY

Søren Kierkegaard was born on 5 May 1813, and few mourned his death forty-two years later in November 1855. Even so, his funeral almost ended in a small riot over whether he should be buried by the church against his wishes.

Søren was the youngest of seven children, and his mother was his father's second wife, previously the first wife's maid. His father's first wife died childless after being married for two years. Before Søren was even nine years old, one brother and one sister had died. His two surviving sisters, a brother, and his mother all died before he was twenty-one. He was convinced he would not live to be more than thirty-three. Søren's father died at age eighty-one, when

Søren was twenty-five. His father had much influence upon him, yet much of this was experienced as oppressive. (His relation to his father was complex, oscillating between feeling deprived of his childhood to feeling guilty for not loving his father enough.)

Kierkegaard was no stranger to death, having witnessed the death of most of his family at such an early age. When he remarked on the temporal nature of existence, on resignation, anxiety, or despair, it was because these themes were close to his own experiences: "I must dare to believe that through Christ I can be saved from the power of depression which I have lived."[3]

Kierkegaard attempted to locate himself in relation to his pseudonyms: "I would place myself higher than Johannes Climacus, lower than Anti-Climacus...Climacus is lower, he denies he is a Christian. Anti-Climacus is higher, a Christian on an extraordinary level."[4] Yet, in *Practice in Christianity*, he considered withdrawing the pseudonym: "I went to the printer. It was too late... So the pseudonym [of Anti-Climacus] was established."[5] As he pointed out, the pseudonym added an impersonal touch, and thus did not belong in *Practice of Christianity*.[6]

Although Kierkegaard was at times conflicted about the idea of writing under pseudonyms, it is only too obvious that he never wrote as if he were absent; rather, he is in evidence on every page we read. More generally, the pseudonyms often express Kierkegaard's own thoughts, frustrations, and even his experiences. In one work he describes an imaginary character who is never happy, has no friends, no love, and thinks there will be no grief at his death.[7] Another imaginary construction, Johannes Climacus, also resembles Kierkegaard: he is portrayed as an alien, an outsider, and a stranger, removed and disinterested.[8] In fact, Johannes Climacus is described in terms that could well apply to Kierkegaard himself:

> He felt pressure; it was as if forceps had to be used in his youth when he was delivered into the world, as if he were still wanting to slip back; he was not born easily and thus did not come into the world smiling and victorious, as if everything were merely waiting for him.[9]

In Kierkegaard's own eyes, he never had a childhood. He thought of himself as born old.[10] Even his schoolmates remarked how he always dressed in a relatively serious and "adult" manner for a child. He always perceived himself as old, deformed, or physically unfit. Some have even argued that he had a hunchback, although there is no evidence for this claim. It could be imagined that he walked as if he did have one due to his own self-perception. On 25 September 1855, he remarked, "Through a crime I came into existence...I came into existence against God's will."[11] His constant complaint that he had never lived, never been a man, even less had a childhood, resonates in his idea that he was born old.

Furthermore, in his journals he "imagines" a man walking who would not care if something fell from the sky and killed him. Kierkegaard's own personal journal tells of the exact same sentiment pertaining to himself. In short, he often took his personal experiences and transferred them to his imaginary characters. (Nonetheless, Kierkegaard was of the opinion that the authorship of his work should be attributed to mankind at large, as to express the universal applicability of the psychology he elucidated.)

We would not have fully considered Søren Kierkegaard's personal life unless we were to mention his infamous engagement to Regine Olsen. He courted this seventeen-year-old girl, and succeeded in becoming engaged to her. In some sense all Kierkegaard's voluptuous writings are love letters to her, although he saw this work in a larger perspective: as part of his quest for the "religious," and hence his attempt to break with "the world," with Regine. He broke his engagement with Regine, although she begged him not to. When she asked him what he was going to do, he cruelly remarked that he intended to "sow his wild oats"—and perhaps write. The first was a patent lie, which he used strategically to push Regine away from him; after returning home he did nothing but cry. Later he was to remark: "When I left her I chose death."[12] Although, for a short time, he openly admitted his regret at breaking the engagement, he soon saw it as a necessary step on his path. He had already stated that becoming an author required "sacrificing everything," and he had already developed the habit of retreating from the world, so it is no surprise that post-Regine, women would become his symbol for the world, for temporality, and stand in opposition to the spirit world of ideas. He wrote: "If I had faith, I would have stayed with Regine. Thanks to God I now see that. I have been on the point of losing my mind these days."[13] The personal reason why Kierkegaard broke off his engagement, in my view, was his fear of bringing someone such as Regine, innocent and beautiful, into his dark life, his melancholy, his depression. Kierkegaard says that, spiritually speaking, everything is possible. Yet his engagement to Regine showed that he did not really believe everything was in fact possible; it forced him to realize his lack of faith. He considered a successful relationship with Regine as an impossibility:

> I would have to initiate her into terrible things, my relationship to my father, his melancholy, the eternal night brooding within me, my going astray, my lusts and debauchery, which, however, in the eyes of God are perhaps not so glaring; for it was, after all, anxiety that made me go astray, and where was I to seek a safe stronghold when I knew or suspected that the only man I had admired for his strength was tottering.[14]

Not only was Kierkegaard worried about introducing Regine to his life, but he admits that it was anxiety that made him seek a safe foundation when the only man he admired, his father, that austere authoritarian, was "tottering."

He is at odds with his own philosophy and life, since it is anxiety that made him go astray, yet is precisely that which is the key in his theory of the self. In his philosophy, it will be anxiety that acts as the main conduit for human development toward the religious. If we are not to see his flight from temporal life to the eternal as an attempted cure for constant anxiety, in which case this progression is undertaken on mistaken grounds, we have to mitigate his remark. That is to say, we have to suggest that Kierkegaard had an ambivalent attitude toward his life. On the one hand, there is acceptance of being an instrument of God, a martyr and an author; on the other hand, there is regret over Regine and over never taking up a profession.

Kierkegaard understood himself, at the most basic level, as a melancholy person. His idea that he was old played into his further notion that he did not fit in: someone who is "old" cannot easily fit in with playmates. Indeed, as a child he was an outsider, and he remained one his entire life. On numerous occasions, he would speak of himself as a ghost, of belonging to the world of spirits and ideas, not "the world," and always being outside of himself. It has been remarked that he lived in his body as one lives in a rented room. His body was that of a runt, which he had to deal with as a sort of luggage. The idea of estrangement, alienation, is present again in his elucidation of Johannes Climacus:

> His comments would not meet with sympathy. It was impossible for him to speak as the others did, and, on the other hand, he realized very well that the others would not understand him...For a moment it pained him that once again he was not like the others, but soon forgot the pain in the joy of thinking.[15]

Kierkegaard was the outsider who could not enjoy life as others did, seemingly carefree and happy. Yet, his imaginary pseudonym could find quietude in thinking, and Kierkegaard in writing. We get a glimpse into his mental life, from his writing of May 1839:

> I live in my room as one besieged—I prefer to see no one, and every moment I fear that the enemy will try an assault—that is, someone will come and visit me...I cry myself tired...I say of my sorrow what the Englishman says of his house: My sorrow is my castle...I live and feel these days somewhat as a chess man must feel when the opponent says: That piece cannot be moved—like a useless spectator...[16]

He had a fear of "others," yet he was lonely. His constant sorrow was the one thing by which he knew himself; it was his "castle."

Kierkegaard's entire psychological orientation toward the world rendered him a spectator. In his position of spectator, he felt a crippling paralysis. At one point he wrote: "I feel like a spider that preserves its life by remaining overlooked in its corner, although it shivers and quakes inwardly with presentiments of a storm...My thought and its fate are not of the slightest importance to anyone, with the exception of myself."[17] And, in the same vein, "A secret anxiety broods over my whole inner being, an oppressiveness that forebodes an earthquake."[18]

Again, the idea that he was constantly oppressed by some anxiety or deep pathos fits well with his self-perception as old, melancholy, and in a constant sorrow, his "castle": "Now I dive down once again into the depths—and there

I hide myself; I envelop myself within myself—I live on depression."[19] At times he described his mood as a theatre after everyone has left, empty. In this connection, he complained of reaching a type of despair in which he could not even feel sadness, his one loyal friend. "The only thing I see is emptiness; the only thing I live on is emptiness, the only thing I move in is emptiness—I do not even suffer pain...my soul is like the Dead Sea, over which no bird is able to fly; when it has come midway, it sinks down in a stupor to death and destruction."[20]

Anxiety serves a positive, instrumental purpose in human development within Kierkegaard's philosophy. Anxiety, like the other points of meditation for Kierkegaard, was not foreign to him:

> All existence makes me anxious, from the smallest fly to the mysteries of the Incarnation; the whole thing is inexplicable to me, I myself most of all; to me all existence is infected. I myself most of all. My distress is enormous, boundless; no one knows it except God in heaven, and he will not console me; no one can console me except God in heaven, and he will not take compassion on me.[21]

The essential nature of Kierkegaard's anxiety remains elusive. He was not anxious over this or that thing, an event in the past or possible future, but just anxious in general. In fact, the reason he was anxious was that he was not confronted with a clearly defined problem that he could rationally deal with. For instance, if we are worried about an examination we have to write, we can take care to prepare well, and thus quell our anxiety. But Kierkegaard was anxious about everything and nothing. If I were to locate a more specific cause of his anxiety, I would still be forced to speak in very general terms. He was anxious about his place in the world, in the universe at large as well as in the human world (community): "Deep within every human being there still lives the anxiety over the possibility of being alone in the world, forgotten by God, overlooked among the millions and millions in this enormous household."[22]

Johannes Climacus writes of his standing as an author, "I am so insignificant that I am an outsider in literature. I have not even added to subscription literature, nor can it truthfully be said that I have a significant place in it."[23] In his own day, he sees a trade of inauthentic authors and "two-bit reviewers" and wrote: "A genuine author means a sacrificed life..."[24] The first lines of *Fear and Trembling* begin by stating that "Not only in the business world but also in the world of ideas, our age stages a real sale." He made it clear that one should not write aspiring to become famous, "noticed, recognized or praised,"[25] as women adorning themselves, but that an author is best to have no readers or perhaps only five "genuine readers."[26] Kierkegaard sums up his view of his contemporaries in literature like this:

> If it were conceivable that one could become an author without writing, could purchase this dignity just as one buys a title, yet, please note, actually enjoying a bit of a reputation—then a great many of the authors of our

generation would perhaps stop writing. And if one could, without doing any writing, earn the money one earns writing, then many contemporary authors would undoubtedly refrain from writing, and we would see how many genuine authors we do have.[27]

Furthermore, Kierkegaard confirmed that some of what he wrote under the cloak of his pseudonyms was applicable to himself, as we can tell by consulting his journal: "Assigned from childhood to a life of torment that perhaps few even conceive of, plunged into the deepest despondency, and from this despondency again into despair, I came to understand myself by writing."[28] Kierkegaard says:

> [B]efore God I regard my whole work as an author as my own education. I am not a teacher but a learner...But I have not said that I, measured against every part-time teacher, could not be called a teacher, but that before God, measured against the ideals for being a teacher, I call myself a learner...[29]

According to Kierkegaard, the writer must sacrifice his life. Not surprisingly, his icons Christ and Socrates were both martyrs of a sort. In fact, he also at times considered himself a martyr. This was perhaps his most resonant understanding of his life. That is to say, if he had been asked what his "purpose" was, he would himself have been amazed at how well God had shaped him for his task as poet, Christian thinker, philosopher, the writer-martyr, and ultimately to be himself.

Kierkegaard's purest intentions are transferred to the reader. In his writings, he often refers to his "reader" or "dear reader."[30] (He perhaps hoped that this reader would read him out loud, as if he was writing one of those sermons he was so fond of reading in his earlier days.) Kierkegaard worried that none of his readers would understand what we can call his "total plan" (from Danish: *total-anlæg*), which underlies all his various pseudonyms. He writes:

> There will be no judgment at all on my authorship in its totality, for no one had sufficient faith in it or time or competence to look for a comprehensive plan [Total-Anleog] in the entire production. Consequently the verdict will be that I have changed somewhat over the years. So it will be. This distresses me. I am deeply convinced that there is an integral coherence, that there is a comprehensiveness in the whole production.[31]

Also, he hoped that his reader was "like me," whom he characterized as "dead"; not having died, but rather not having lived. Søren Kierkegaard's last name translates to "churchyard" or "cemetery." Perhaps this is the best image for the tone of his life.

His one goal, ultimately, was to be "saved" from his suffering; however, he saw this salvation only as an effect of achieving his goal: "If only I myself manage to be just a simple Christian...I must dare to believe that through

Christ I can be saved from the power of depression in which I have lived..."[32] In the end, Kierkegaard did not feel he ever became "a Christian" (something he raved against so-called Christians for never attaining.) He lived to produce, to write; or, put differently, his writing allowed him to live, while he felt that the Christian thing to do was not to produce but to exist. This is some of the reason why his journal writing waned toward the very end of his life; he was gradually ceasing to produce.

Kierkegaard suggested a possible way: "Psychology is what we need, and, above all, thorough knowledge of human life as well as sympathy for its interests. Herein lies the task, and until this is resolved there can be no question of completing a Christian view of life."[33] He wanted to understand what it truly means to be a human being in order to know how to live, in order to be ethical. Psychology, then, becomes central to a Christian ethics, for we cannot know how to live if we do not know who we are. Again, we return to Kierkegaard's psychological quest to know himself, which he represented as having both a Socratic and Christian motif.

The motivation for many renowned psychologists has been the quest to *know thyself*. It is well known, for example, that Sigmund Freud's self-analysis was a motivation behind his work, and Carl Jung's self-exploration or search for himself was extensive. Kierkegaard was no different in this respect.

That the themes of many of Kierkegaard's works are psychological is evident by the titles or subtitles of his books: *The Concept of Anxiety* is subtitled "A Simple Psychologically Oriented Deliberation..."; a subtitle in *Stages on Life's Way* is "An imaginary psychological construction"; "...Development of Personality" is a section in *Either/Or II*; "A Christian Psychological Exposition..." is the subtitle of *Sickness unto Death*, and *Repetition* is called "A Venture in Experimenting Psychology." In fact, in 1881, Georg Brandes wrote a letter to Nietzsche commenting that Kierkegaard was one of the most profound psychologists who ever lived.[34]

MODERN LOSS

Kierkegaard notes, in *The Practice of Christianity*, that we usually act in relation to an established authority. We have to look out for our interests, which may require keeping those who hold the keys in good spirits.[35] We would like to think that our position in the world is consistent with having a God-relationship. Yet, the God-relationship may in fact be at odds with our position (which may require heeding customs antithetical to the personal relationship to God we seek).[36] Having two masters may not work, especially when fitting in with one's fellows represents, as he saw it, the elusive security of the temporal world: "My whole view, which I have always avowed, is that the evil is not the government but the crowd."[37]

A passage from *The Present Age*, completed in 1846, reads: "Our age is essentially one of understanding and reflection, without passion, momentarily bursting into enthusiasm, and shrewdly relapsing into repose."[38] His complaint in this instance is that his age never reaches action, but remains alienated from the world.

Nowadays not even a suicide kills himself in desperation. Before taking the step he deliberates so long and so carefully that he literally chokes with thought. It is even questionable whether he ought to be called suicide, since it is really thought which takes his life. He does not die with deliberation but from deliberation. It would therefore be very difficult to prosecute the present generation because of its legal quibbles: in fact, all its ability, virtuosity and good sense consists in trying to get a judgment and a decision without ever getting as far as action.[39]

The effect of reflection that remains, as it were, in our heads is a type of paralysis. And the age is, according to Kierkegaard, utterly lost in reflection.

Thus our own age is essentially one of understanding, and on the average, perhaps, more knowledgeable than any former generation, but it is without passion. Every one knows a great deal, we all know which way we ought to go and all the different ways we can go, but nobody is willing to move. If at last some one were to overcome the reflection within him and happened to act, then immediately thousands of reflections would form an outward obstacle. Only a proposal to reconsider a plan is greeted with enthusiasm; action is met with indolence.[40]

It is not that he considered reflection bad in itself, but he did find it reprehensible when its proportions nullified acting.[41] As he said:

Reflection is not evil; but a reflective condition and the deadlock which it involves, by transforming the qualities which precede action into a means of escape from action, is both corrupt and dangerous and leads in the end to a retrograde movement.[42]

We are reduced to the status of spectators, which, if we recall, Kierkegaard always felt he was. He speaks of the inability to act: "A revolutionary age is an age of action: Ours is the age of advertisement and publicity."[43]

Kierkegaard regards the notion of "the public" as an abstraction: it lacks reality, in much the same way everyday life lacks reality and purpose. He writes:

Only when the sense of association in society is no longer strong enough to give life to concrete realities is the Press able to create that abstraction "the Public," consisting of unreal individuals who never are and never can be united in an actual situation or organization—and yet are held together as a whole.[44]

While admitting that society was in possession of a great deal of technical know-how, Kierkegaard asked, somewhat rhetorically, what "knowing" really meant.[45] As he so succinctly put it, what would be the point of having explained the whole world and yet not understand myself?

Since Kierkegaard viewed the crowd as reinforcing the tendency of inauthentic individuals who reflect "without passion, momentarily bursting into enthusiasm, and shrewdly relapsing into repose," we can begin to construct what Kierkegaard takes the authentic individual to be. Kierkegaard presented two paradigms of authenticity: the genius and the apostle. Both have in common that their reason for action does not lie with the general public, with society at large. Thus, the genius is teleologically oriented, in that he "relates himself to himself" and not, at least primarily, to others. The apostle relates himself to God; and, in fact, acts for God. The apostle has divine "authority" to command the public. So, neither the genius nor the apostle uses the so-called public as their lead. The differences between the two in respect to their relation to the world is that the genius does not write (or act) to affect others, while the apostle's mission is absolutely to affect others.

Aristotle remarked that men began to philosophize out of wonder. However, Kierkegaard clearly philosophizes out of dread. His work allows us to characterize him as part of the romantic reaction against (aspects of) modernity. In the first place, he emphasizes subjectivity. Also, he sees the mass age as an inauthentic response to our common sickness (emblemized, according to him, in the established church). And, of course, his conception of the self is teleological.

Admittedly, he does differ from the romantic poets, for example, in his demotion of the temporal world. Also, his attempt to write subjectively is often overshadowed by his use of pseudonyms, which, paradoxically, seem to objectify human existence. It could be argued that if he were serious about subjectivity he would have written only autobiographically (notwithstanding that subjectivity pervades his pseudonyms).

Kierkegaard's most profound mistake, perhaps, is to seek his foundation outside of temporal existence. It is the search outside temporality that leads to his ascetic denial of the world, and leads him to claim: all is nothing...smoke in the wind. We need not deny that within the framework of Kierkegaard's creation, it is better to be ethical than to be a seducer, for example. Yet, there may be other ways in which to find fulfilment that do not require his degradation of the temporal world. More specifically, his emphasis on the God-relationship seems to have put him into conflict with his fellow human beings, which induces scepticism regarding the possibility of realizing the love for others (other than Kierkegaard's Republic) that is the earthly token of the religious life.

I have not offered a sustained criticism of Kierkegaard's solution. Rather, I have pointed out that his solution may not be optimal; Aristotle, for example, would probably not think Kierkegaard's solution moderate enough to be optimal. Nor does Kierkegaard's own life, after all, seem a desirable model for human existence. His thinking may reflect a particular historical situation relating to modernity. Concern over the plausibility of Kierkegaard's solution prompts us to at least consider various attempts to locate the ground of the self within a socio-historical context, where finding fulfilment in harmonious relations with others is emphasized. In what follows I therefore consider the self from a sociological point of view.

2

THE
SOCIOLOGICAL SELF

~ 6 ~

ROUSSEAU

BORN IN 1772, Rousseau is famous for his treatise on education, *Émile*, and the *Social Contract*, where he seems to defend individual autonomy from the imposition of society; thus, he has often been thought a romantic. In Rousseau's account of the self we witness the tension between a theological and social conception of the self.

Though for Rousseau development seems to follow a fall from grace, it is, in the end, the only way of becoming fully human. The ground of the self is realized in social relations, built around a remnant core of a theological conception much like Kierkegaard's. Rousseau seems to find inspiration equally in history and theology. The difference from Kierkegaard, I argue, is one of degree and not kind. Rousseau emphasizes the social element of the self, to which Kierkegaard makes little reference.

Rousseau seems at first glance to be juxtaposed to Kierkegaard. Yet, we need to investigate if the picture of juxtaposition is deceptive. In this chapter, we shall see how Rousseau and Kierkegaard have much more in common than is otherwise thought. I begin with Rousseau's account of the self.

NATURE

According to Rousseau, "It is only by movement that we learn the difference between self and not self."[1] Rousseau fought against the practice of wrapping babies in swaddling cloths because they restricted their movements. Rousseau comments, "Civilized man is born and dies a slave...All his life long man is imprisoned by our institutions."[2] Even in infancy, in Rousseau's eyes, natural movement is constricted.

Rousseau's criticism of human institutions spills over in harsh words against many established organizations that restrict nature. For example, he levels the following critique against medical practices:

> I do not know what the doctors cure us of, but I know this: they infect us with very deadly diseases, cowardice, timidity, credulity, the fear of death. What matter it they make the dead walk, we have no need of corpses...Medicine is all the fashion these days, and very naturally. It is the amusement of the idle and unemployed, who do not know what to

do with their time, and so spend it in taking care of themselves...Such men must have doctors to threaten and flatter them, to give them the only pleasure they can enjoy, the pleasure of not being dead...I do not deny that medicine is useful to some men; I assert that it is fatal to mankind...give us medicine without doctors, for when we have both, the blunders of the artist are a hundredfold greater than our hopes from the art...as I never call in a doctor for myself, I will never send for one for Émile, unless his life is clearly in danger, when the doctor will but kill him.[3]

Another of Rousseau's attacks on society is centred on the illegitimate desires he claims it instils in us. For instance:

It is one of the misfortunes of the rich to be cheated on all sides; what wonder they think ill of mankind! It is riches that corrupt men, and the rich are rightly the first to feel the defects of the only tool they know. Everything is ill-done for them, except what they do themselves, and they do next to nothing.[4]

Many of our vices Rousseau considers as results of the societal impositions made on us. For example, he is a critic of urbanization (moving away from nature) as contributing to the vices of high society (e.g., materialism).[5]

As humankind moves forward through history, Rousseau sees it becoming more technological in satisfying its needs. The technological progress of man, however, promotes ever new needs, ever greedier desires, hence, ironically, leading to less rather than more satisfaction. Also, as we move toward what is popularly termed civilization, we are increasingly alienated from nature and feeling. Rousseau finds technological estrangement to be emblemized by the written word that stands to eliminate all the feeling in such rudimentary forms of communication as poetry: "The study of philosophy and the progress of reason, while having perfected grammar, deprive language of its vital, passionate quality which made it so singable."[6] Feeling is taken as primitive, as is poetry, and it is only with development of reason, logic, and grammar that a large part of feeling is expunged from language.[7] Furthermore, he takes the spoken word to precede the written word. (The spoken word, hence, contains more feeling.)

He believes language to be integral to being human,[8] but writes of natural man, "Such intercourse did not require a language much more refined than that of crows or monkeys, which group together in approximately the same way."[9] It is by acquiring linguistic abilities, however, that reflection, according to Rousseau, is possible: "Speech distinguishes man among the animals."[10] What exactly Rousseau means by language remains obscure (since he admits that even bees have a natural language). The distinguishing feature of humans, however, is that language is learned.[11]

Rousseau speaks of the origin of language:

It is neither hunger nor thirst, but love, hatred, pity, anger, which drew from them the first words. Fruit does not disappear from our hands. One can take nourishment without speaking. One stalks in silence the prey on which one would feast. But for moving a young heart, or repelling an unjust aggressor, nature dictates accents, cries, lamentations.[12]

Rousseau believed that feelings were what elicited the first sounds that were to form themselves into words. Before language, he tells us, there was only feeling: "One does not begin by reasoning but by feeling."[13]

The first stage of social development, in Rousseau's hypothetical anthropology, is referred to as the savage state. In the savage state, man uses only the most rudimentary forms of communication, such as the depiction of objects (as in hieroglyphics). The second stage of development is termed the barbaric, and its linguistic corollary consists of propositions and conventional characters "that can be done only when the language is completely formed and an entire people is united by common laws."[14] In the third stage, which he calls civilization, language admits of analysis in its elementary parts, in other words of a grammar, which is conventional and standardized. Rousseau's tripartite theory of social evolution can be summed up as consisting of the following stages: the savage (feeling), the barbaric (reflection), and the civilized (formalization). The direction of progress is from what is private, such as feeling, to what is social and conventional, that is, language. Rousseau took an interest in the origin of languages because of its possible connection to the origin of "human institutions."[15]

Rousseau hypothesizes on pre-societal man: "The natural man lives for himself; he is the unit, the whole, dependent only on himself and on his like."[16] Natural man did not need others: "[W]andering in the forests, without industry, without speech, without domicile, without war and without liaisons, with no need of his fellowmen..."[17]

In Rousseau's imaginary anthropology of natural man, men come together because of weakness and suffering: "A really happy man is a hermit; God only enjoys absolute happiness."[18] By ourselves we are independent, and it is here that Rousseau pictures ideal happiness (that is why he grants being alone only to God). He writes, "When man is content to be himself he is strong indeed; when he strives to be more than man he is weak indeed."[19] Society, according to Rousseau, breeds a weakness in mankind in that it increases our needs (and hence our dependence).[20] Rousseau identifies two types of dependence, that upon things and people. It is dependence upon people, in his narrative, which is said to give rise to all other vices.[21]

Conversely, the child (like the natural man) has feeling, but does not possess reason. Rousseau endows his natural man with a sense of pity, for instance.[22] Pity is the morality of natural man before it is replaced by convention, custom, and law. It is pity that moderates natural man's self-interest. Rousseau writes:

> His fellow-man can be murdered with impunity right under his window; he has only to put his hands over his ears and argue with himself a bit to prevent nature...Savage man does not have this admirable talent, and

> for want of wisdom and reason he is always seen heedlessly yielding
> to the first sentiment of humanity...[P]ity is a natural sentiment which,
> moderating in each individual the activity of love of oneself...[23]

When we entered the societal phase and began to be concerned about what others thought of us, this concern became the primary vehicle of social control:

> Each one began to look at the others and to want to be looked at himself,
> and public esteem had a value...and it was no longer possible to be
> disrespectful towards anyone with impunity. From this came the first
> duties of civility, even among the savages...The offended man saw in
> it contempt for his person which was often more unbearable than the
> harm itself.[24]

According to Rousseau, in society we attempt to please others, and to avoid their contempt, and in so doing, conform ourselves to the wills of others. The birth of social conventions is set against the pre-social state of natural man: "But the social order is a sacred right that serves as a basis for all the others. However, this right does not come from nature; it is therefore based on conventions."[25]

Rousseau offers some possible reasons for why people come to live in societies (even though this leads to much repression, hypocrisy, and inauthenticity). Survival is the first imperative,[26] one not much stressed by Rousseau, however, due to his conception of nature as a veritable Eden. The second reason for giving up freedom for civil society is the aspiration to private property.[27]

Rousseau tends at times to speak as if his state of nature was amoral. Morality proper (i.e., not mere pity) is seen to be an imposition by society. He writes:

> One who dares to undertake the founding of a people should feel that he
> is capable of changing human nature, so to speak; of transforming each
> individual, who by himself is a perfect and solitary whole, into a part of
> a larger whole...substituting a partial and moral existence for the physical
> and independent existence we have all received from nature.[28]

The characteristics Rousseau attributes to natural man are: independence, entirety, freedom, happiness, and (at times) self-interest. By entirety, Rousseau wishes to indicate that man in his natural state is complete. Yet, according to Rousseau, natural man's abilities are realized at a higher level, as it were, in civil society. For every loss there is at least the possibility of a gain. In civil society, self-interest, for instance, undergoes "substitution."

In civil society, according to Rousseau, we are not purely self-interested but, rather, absorbed in a general will. He argues that since others also submit to this general will, one is submitting to oneself.[29] The idea is to collapse ourselves into the group, so that we could say that if everyone wants what the group wants, the group wants what each individual wants.[30] For instance, Rousseau claims that even to die for the state is in the individual's interest (since the individual's interest becomes synonymous with the state's interests).[31] According to Rousseau, the law cannot be considered unjust to the individual, since it can never, in principle, be against her interest (though, theoretically, if it was not in the interest of the public, it could be "unjust").[32] Although we may even have to sacrifice our lives for the state, the reason civil society is preferable to a state of nature is the possibility it offers us of becoming fully human.[33]

Rousseau's theory of human development is mirrored in his categories for political regimes, where he sees three types of governance: monarchy (submission to ourselves), government (submission to the parent), and democracy (submission to society). The monarchy is run by someone, a prince, who only cares for his own interests (thus resembling the natural man). However, of democracy Rousseau writes, "Individuals having only submitted themselves to the sovereign, and the sovereign power being only the general will, we shall see that every man in obeying the sovereign only obeys himself and how much freer are we under the social pact than in the state of nature."[34]

Rousseau understands man to have a second nature. Much of what we are is acquired. He writes:

> God makes all things good; man meddles with them and they become evil. He forces one soil to yield the products of another, one tree to bear another's fruit. He confuses and confounds time, place, and natural conditions. He mutilates his dog, his horse, and his slave. He destroys and defaces all things; he loves all that is deformed and monstrous; he will have nothing as nature made it, not even man himself, who must learn his paces like a saddle-horse, and be shaped to his master's taste like the trees in his garden. Yet things would be worse without this education...[35]

Human beings require education. (Rousseau, though having written a treatise on raising children, *Émile*, had put his own five children in foundling homes.) Nevertheless he writes, "But I think I have clearly perceived the material which is to be worked upon."[36] That is to say, he claims to have understood human nature.[37] We only become human by our exposure to society.

MORALITY

Ethics do not apply to man in his original and natural state. Historically, all the vices we have accrued are subsequent to entering into society; that is, social institutions are held responsible for corrupting the nature of man. Also, by definition, ethics involve relations to others (which do not exist in the natural state).

Rousseau recognizes, however, what he calls three masters: nature, things, and men. Knowledge of things cannot be instructive in relation to morality.[38] Morality is primarily about our relations to others. Rousseau's fictional pupil, Émile, for example, only becomes concerned about morality at the age of fifteen. Only at fifteen does Émile begin to have relations with others (in any significant sense). Rousseau writes, "As soon as man needs a companion he is no longer an isolated creature, his heart is no longer alone."[39] It is at the time of puberty that Rousseau sees the need for others arise, a need that results in an interaction that inaugurates us into a moral world.

As Émile grows, he attains the ability for doubt through reflection. Rousseau claims, for instance, that with maturity we can become doubters and sceptics. We enter into the social world much like Émile, who reaches that age where he is to go outside of the family. In Rousseau's fictional anthropology we are brought together not by a sovereign or external need—at least not primarily—but by our inner moral nature that requires others. If we are only human by language, as Rousseau maintains, and language requires a social context, the deduction is clear: humans require a social context to be fully human.

Rousseau, himself, ridicules the idea of a natural man, since it raises obvious questions. If we were all alone, where did we come from? As Rousseau puts it:

> What then! Before that time did men spring from the earth? Did generations succeed each other without any union of the sexes, and without anyone being understood? No: there were families, but there were no nations. There were domestic languages, but there were no popular ones...[40]

Also, a human infant could not survive long without the aid of other humans, and could not learn language without them. Rousseau indicates, therefore, that the state of nature was a social condition in which we lived in a close-knit, incestuous family, with no recourse to other people (who either did not exist or were not known to exist).

We cannot realize our status as full human beings in isolation because it gives us no opportunity to exercise our abilities:

> Again, if, as it is impossible to doubt, man is by nature sociable, or at least fitted to become sociable, he can only be so by means of other innate feelings, relative to his kind...the motive power of conscience is derived from the moral system formed through this twofold relation to himself and to his fellow man...[41]

Rousseau speaks of being "fitted to become social." Man inherently has feelings, such as pity (and conscience), which draw us together (and govern our behaviour), but these feelings are, according to Rousseau, refined and perfected only in a social context.

Morality is not based upon reason, however. Rousseau remarks: "Conscience! Conscience! Divine instinct, immortal voice from above."[42] Conscience is taken to be a feeling that precedes all judgement. Rousseau writes:

> The most unworthy gods were worshipped by the noblest men. The sacred voice of nature stronger than the voice of the gods...There is therefore at the bottom of our hearts an innate principle of justice and virtue...it is this principle that I call conscience.[43]

Even if the gods command us to perform unethical acts (as in Abraham's case), Rousseau is convinced that morality is so natural to man that we are capable of ethical behaviour even under considerable strain. Yet, "Reason alone is not sufficient foundation for virtue; what solid ground can be found? Virtue we are told is love of order... If there is no God, the wicked is right and the good man is nothing but a fool."[44] Ethics is grounded metaphysically in the idea of nature, which is, in turn, guaranteed by God.[45] It is, therefore, because man fully becomes himself only through morality that Émile is brought to live in society.[46]

THE SOCIAL BEING

Durkheim interprets Rousseau as having a social conception of man.[47] He considers the hypothesis of the natural man to have been a thought experiment used to tease out which of mankind's tendencies and abilities might be present prior to social existence.[48]

Downplaying the idea of pity and conscience, Durkheim also maintains that Rousseau sees the social sense as being contingent upon a social context. Durkheim claims that this social sense is emergent. He explicitly argues against the commonly held view that Rousseau would have considered the state of nature to be where the perfection of man was attained, while society and civilization could add nothing but corruption. On a teleological reading of the sociological school, man in fact perfects himself in society. Durkheim writes:

> *The Social Contract* becomes unintelligible, for if society as such is an evil, our sole concern with it should be an endeavour to reduce its development to a minimum, and we are at a loss to understand all Rousseau's effort to provide it with a positive organization. Particularly the importance he attaches to collective discipline and his subordination, in certain respects, of the individual become quite inexplicable.[49]

Durkheim goes on to argue that Rousseau would not have proposed that we not only join a society but also submit ourselves to the majority if he hadn't had a social conception of man. On Durkheim's interpretation, all of man's innate abilities and faculties flourish in the social state (up until then having lain dormant).[50] Just as man has the capacity for language, morality, and so on, it is only in the social context that these things emerge and flower.[51]

More recently, Charles Taylor has added weight to Durkheim's interpretation by challenging the traditional individualistic reading of Rousseau.[52] Rousseau is usually taken to be a proponent of the notion that we are authentic as individuals (and unauthentic when we depend on others' recognition). When we depend on others, seemingly, our actions, become formed in such a way as to please those on whom we depend, rather than taking shape based on our own will.

Taylor points out, however, that Rousseau only claims that recognition by others leads to inauthenticity in a non-egalitarian society (as we would be submitting ourselves to an elite rather than to the general will).[53] In an egalitarian society, however, to be recognized by others is consistent with Rousseau's political belief that we should submit ourselves to the general will. The idea, according to Taylor, is that by doing what others want you are also being authentic (in an egalitarian society). What Taylor's interpretation of Rousseau has brought to the fore, then, is the notion that ethical behaviour has some limiting factors, such as freedom from extreme forms of oppression.[54] Taylor's reading of Rousseau provides the basis for social action to confront injustice.

Struggle between two idealized visions, the individual utopia and the social prison, form a tension within Rousseau's edifice, and in romantic thought in general. Alone man cannot be human. Yet, the social gives birth to inequality and hypocrisy. Rousseau's solution is to paint a picture in which certain emergent properties—such as morality—can flourish in a (just) social context.

Compared to Kierkegaard, for instance, the emphasis in presentation has shifted (away from a discussion of God), but his thought had not been eclipsed. Rousseau's three stages of development (indicated in parentheses) fit into two of Kierkegaard's: (i) self-interest (the aesthete), followed by (ii) reflection, and leading to (iii) formalization (the ethical man). Kierkegaard's God-relationship, the religious stage, is absent from Rousseau's discourse on the self.

Rousseau's conception of the self, we may wish to note, is nonetheless in the romantic tradition. The solitude Kierkegaard seeks with God, Rousseau finds in nature. For Rousseau, we leave the mythical state of nature to exist in a society. For Kierkegaard, we leave an aesthetic existence to build a relationship with God. For both Kierkegaard and Rousseau, self-development comes at an inevitable price. Also, for both thinkers, ethics is perceived as the fruit of teleological development.

In chapter 5, I suggested that Kierkegaard's portrait of the self requires emendation. Studying Rousseau beckons us to add some needed detail to Kierkegaard's thoughts on ethics, and hence on what a self is. Specifically, though ethics one way or another concerns others, for Kierkegaard it is a by-product of the Aristotelian quest to become the ideal person. Rousseau acknowledges, or at least emphasizes, more radically that our relations to others are part of who we are. Our conception of our limitations and aspirations— those two poles of the self discussed in chapter 1—are partly defined by the social context in which we find ourselves. Education, in Rousseau's rudimentary sense, is the *sine qua non* of becoming a person.

The notion that God defined man's nature takes on a new hue in Rousseau's thought. According to Rousseau, we are *meant* to be social beings. The theological tone, I suggest, would lie, though more deeply buried, underneath nineteenth-century sociological thought.

It was imperative to investigate whether or not the perception of Rousseau's juxtaposition to Kierkegaard is deceptive. This chapter shows them to have more in common than one might originally have surmised.

7

DURKHEIM

I SHALL DETAIL Durkheim's account of the self as a reflection of society, whereby the theological underpinnings, discussed earlier, recede into the background. Durkheim, the founder of the first school of sociological thought, shares with the romantics a critique of modernity. Yet, he differs from Kierkegaard, for instance, by rejecting the equation of individuality with authenticity. He falls just shy of losing the self in history.

Moving further away from Rousseau, Durkheim seems to mark an obvious break with Kierkegaard. We need to see to what extent, if any, Durkheim's account of the self can complement Kierkegaard's. I begin with Durkheim's sociological approach to the self.

SOCIOLOGIST

Durkheim speaks of two ways in which humans are bound together in a society. On the one hand, mechanical solidarity, he tells us, is where we engage in similar activities, for example, in primitive societies. Organic solidarity, on the other hand, is said to develop by a spontaneous consensus toward a greater division of labour, for example, in industrial societies. When society has farmers, blacksmiths, doctors, and so forth, each depends upon the other.[1] The increasing division of labour, however, has lead to what Durkheim sees as a breakdown of the social fabric of society, where the nature of work in industrial society is often monotonous and uniform.[2]

He notes that the division of labour in modern industrial societies can become too specialized, resulting in an erosion of social solidarity. The person is reduced "to the role of a machine."[3] Durkheim did not think the problems of modernity—for example, alienation—endemic to our predicament, as Kierkegaard suggested, but the result of a transitional period in human history.

Durkheim uses an analogy to illustrate the division of labour. Just as a body has a heart, lungs, and so on, so too is society composed of different parts with specific functions. Consider Durkheim's language in this passage:

> Assuredly murder is always an evil but nothing proves that it is the greatest evil. What does one human being the less matter to society? Or one cell fewer in the organism?[4]

What is valuable is so for society. For Durkheim, since society becomes the sole end of what counts as good, he writes: "In reality the duties of the individual to himself are duties to society."[5]

What we do for a living—that is, how we have been organized—affects what we think. Durkheim writes:

> It is a doubtless self-evident truth that there is nothing in social life that is not in the consciousness of individuals...Most of our states of consciousness...would have occurred completely differently among people grouped together in a different way.[6]

So, our actions are to a large extent determined by society:

> Here it is indeed rather the form of the whole that determines that of the parts. Society does not find ready-made in individual consciousness the bases on which it rests; it makes them for itself.[7]

In fact, as Durkheim puts the situation: "It is not realized that there can be no sociology unless societies exist, and that societies cannot exist if there are only individuals."[8] Durkheim posits a "force," which he refers to as a "thing" or entity, equatable with society.[9] He does not want to give it ontological status, but does say it—society—is "real."[10]

According to Durkheim, when people live together in a group certain patterns of behaviour emerge. These modes of behaviour become customs and eventually laws. "Then the habits as they grow in strength, are transformed into rules of conduct. The past determines the future."[11] How our group socializes us will determine, in large part, who we are to become. Durkheim writes, "Insofar as he belongs to society, the individual transcends himself, both when he thinks and when he acts."[12]

According to Durkheim, the direction of the evolution of society is nevertheless toward increasing power of the social body.[13] For example, according to him, punishments were once private vendettas but are now carried out by law. For Durkheim, law reflects a collective consciousness that maintains a social solidarity.[14] Societies teach us how to respond in given situations, and without this education, each circumstance becomes an upheaval.[15] For Durkheim, humans only exist in societies (although these take various forms).[16] As he puts it, "If to repeat the classic definition, man is a reasonable animal, it is because he is a sociable animal, or at least infinitely more sociable than the other animals."[17]

Durkheim interprets many psychological problems as lack of those things—such as morality—that bind people together. He remarks, for example, that desire is insatiable (goaded on by the imagination), and requires social prohibitions.[18] Durkheim says:

> It is everlastingly repeated that it is man's nature to be eternally dissatisfied, constantly to advance, without relief or rest, toward an indefinite goal. The longing for infinity is daily represented as a mark of moral distinction,

whereas it can only appear within unregulated consciences which elevate to a rule the lack of rule from which they suffer.[19]

In short, our first duty at the present time is to fashion a morality for ourselves. Such a task cannot be improvised in the silence of study...What reflection can and must do is to prescribe the goal that must be attained. That is what we have striven to accomplish.[20]

The loss of older forms of social relations had not been adequately replaced. (Durkheim suggested, for example, that corporations should not be merely economic units but social ones.)

The only thing the sociologist has in common with the world in which she grew up is the desire to be scientific. Nevertheless, in the eighteenth century, when it was popular to see society as a digression from nature, Durkheim viewed society as "the highest expression of nature."[21] Society, far from being unnatural, marks the conditions for the fruition of human nature. On the sociological model, the self finds its ground in a web of social relations.[22] Let us next look at how social relations hold the self in place by considering religion as Durkheim does.[23]

RELIGION

Since the primitive religions are, according to Durkheim, marked by the simplest organizational structure, if we can understand how this structure fashions individuals, we can extrapolate these ideas into more complex social structures.[24] As far as Durkheim is concerned all religions are the same: they all fulfil the same function.[25] He tells us, "Religion is something eminently social." Durkheim is interested in how different social structures, for example, allow various possibilities of thinking (that is, how various religions hold us together in different ways).[26]

The cosmologies offered by religions predate science and philosophy; they not only determined people's knowledge but also the form that knowledge would be elaborated in.[27] Members of primitive religions, for example, often transmitted ideas by telling stories, sometimes expressed in totemism (which he also believes holds a cosmology).[28]

Durkheim's strategy: "A whole cannot be defined except in relation to its part."[29] The constituent parts of a religion are, according to him, the beliefs and rites (or opinions and actions, respectively). Religious beliefs often revolve around a dualism of sacred (real) and profane (worldly).[30] Rites are rules of conduct that dictate how man should comport himself in the face of the sacred.[31]

Durkheim declares religion to be a systematized and lived dream.[32] He begins with the disenchanted world of Newtonian physics and assumes all metaphysical animation is a result of projection. He writes:

Then to explain how the idea of sacredness has been able to take form under these conditions, the majority of the theorists have been obliged to admit that men have superimposed upon reality, such as it is given by observation, an unreal world, constructed entirely out of the fantastic images which agitate his mind during a dream, or else out of the frequently monstrous aberrations produced by the mythological imagination under the bewitching but deceiving influence of language.[33]

Religion often involves a God that baptizes human nature. We are meant to be so-and-so.[34]

Durkheim explains:

> Now it is these things that give man his own place among things; a man is a man only because he is civilized. So he could not escape the feeling that outside of him there are active causes from which he gets the characteristic attributes of his nature and which, as benevolent powers, assist him, protect him and assure him a privileged fate. And of course he must attribute to these powers a dignity corresponding to the great value of the good things he attributes to them.[35]

The superimposition of fantasy upon a Cartesian reality aids in offering a ground for the self. According to Durkheim, religion binds people together, even if it does so by "fabric of errors" rooted in "delusion" and "psychological defects."[36] Durkheim reasons, "a man who did not think with concepts would not be a man because he would not be a social being."[37] Religious institutions organize ideological space for a group of people. Thus, people are bound together in their delirium:

> Moreover, if we give the name delirious to every state in which the mind adds to the immediate data given by the senses and projects its own sentiments and feelings into things, then nearly every collective representation is in a sense delirious; religious beliefs are only one particular case of a very general law.[38]

True to the positivist tradition, Durkheim contends, however, that science portrays the truth, and not just another worldview.[39] (He muses on the fact that Comte thought the idea of "forces" in modern science would disappear because of their mystic origins.)[40] There are, according to Durkheim, false perceptions of the world, shaped by religion, for instance, but also more basic sense impressions, which provide more or less objective data.[41]

SUICIDE

In Durkheim's doctoral dissertation, *The Division of Labour in Society*, he distinguishes mechanical solidarity from its organic counterpart. He was concerned early on about what happens when social bonds erode. Later on in his oeuvre he presented the case of suicide as an example of such erosion.

Durkheim's study of suicide attempts an analysis of the fluctuation of suicide rates. In his investigation, he distinguishes mental illness from suicide (because some age groups may be more prone to mental illness than to suicide). Durkheim writes, "The social suicide-rate therefore bears no definite relation to the tendency to insanity, nor, inductively considered, to the tendency to the various forms of neurasthenia."[42] He suggests, for instance, that the low suicide rates of children and of the very old can be explained by their lack of the social desires the privations of which prompt suicide; they are more self-sufficient.[43] In addition, he believes that men require others to a greater extent than women do, as the former are more complex beings.[44] Durkheim also describes women as being closer to nature (which, to him, explains their lower suicide rates).

What defends us from self-destruction is being part of a society. Durkheim says:

> What constitutes this society is the existence of a certain number of beliefs and practices common to all the faithful, traditional and thus obligatory. The more numerous and strong these collective states of mind are, the stronger the integration of the religious community, and also the greater its preservative value. The details of dogmas and rites are secondary. The essential thing is that they be capable of supporting a sufficiently intense collective life. And because the Protestant church has less consistency than the others it has less moderating effect upon suicide.[45]

The common element in suicide, according to Durkheim, is the lack of social integration in society. He says, "Suicide varies inversely with the degree of integration of the social groups of which the individual forms a part."[46]

Durkheim chronicles three types of suicide (egoistic, altruistic, and anomic):

> Egoistic suicide results from man's no longer finding a basis for existence in life; altruistic suicide, because this basis for existence appears to man situated beyond life itself. The third sort of suicide, the existence of which has been shown, results from man's activities lacking regulation and his consequent sufferings. By virtue of its origin we shall assign this last variety the name of anomic suicide.[47]

Egoistic suicide is defined by excessive individualism (we depend very little upon others). Altruistic suicide is when we kill ourselves out of, for example, a sense of honour. We kill ourselves to be a self. The individual is enveloped by the society such that his interest is assimilated into that of the group. In India, for example, there was a tradition of *suti*: women would burn themselves after their husbands died (sometimes by throwing themselves upon the funeral pyre in a desire to be burned with him).[48] In Japan, part of the warrior tradition of the samurai demanded suicide as a last resort. The Japanese method, incidentally, became institutionalized during the feudal period (1190–1867). The word *seppuku* means "cutting the stomach," and the two Chinese characters it is derived from are pronounced *Hara-Kiri*.[49] The act of what is sometimes referred to as *Hara-Kiri* consisted of stabbing oneself in the stomach (sometimes with a beheading during, or just prior to, the act).

An anomic suicide is the result of the lack of regulation. Anomy can refer to lack of control in the economy, on the domestic level, and so on.[50] A social disintegration may ensue, for example, in the crease between two social orders. This disintegration may lead certain individuals to feel alienated, and result in an increase in suicide rates. The cause of increased suicide is not considered to be decline of the family, but, more generally, social disintegration. Durkheim writes:

> But we have shown that, while religion, the family and the nation are preservatives against egoistic suicide, and the cause of this does not lie in the special sort of sentiments encouraged by each. Rather, they all owe this virtue to the general fact that they are societies and they possess it only in so far as they are well integrated societies; that is, without excess in one direction or the other.[51]

The greater cohesion in a society the fewer suicides (given the qualification that excessive cohesion can lead to altruistic suicides).

Durkheim allows that there may be individual anomalies to his theory (such as personal tragedy). Individual suicides, however, still bear a "collective mark."[52] Durkheim states, "The private experiences usually thought to be the proximate causes of suicide have only the influence borrowed from the victim's moral predisposition, itself an echo of the moral state of society."[53] He goes on, "The productive cause of the phenomenon naturally escapes the observer of individuals only; for it lies outside individuals. To discover it, we must raise his point of view above individual suicides and perceive what gives them unity."[54]

Durkheim posits two generic types of suicides: ones having to do with exaggerated socialization and identification (altruism), and ones where there is a marked alienation (egoism and anomism). He also grants that some suicides may be a result of a pull in both directions.[55] The solution, more generally, is (the correct amount of) solidarity. Durkheim writes:

> [H]e will no longer find the only aim of his conduct in himself, and, understanding that he is the instrument of a purpose greater than himself, he will see that he is not without significance. Life will resume meaning in his eyes, because it will recover its natural aim and orientation.[56]

Yet, Durkheim is not optimistic about our ability to return to the past as that would conflict with free thought. That is to say, if social integration is to occur, it must be sought in a new type of organization, not merely in mimicking, for example, a feudal past.[57]

At any rate, altruistic suicide is easily distinguishable from the other varieties. It is not clear, however, what the difference between egoistic and anomic suicide is (since they both involve a lack of social integration).[58] Durkheim has already admitted that they spring from the same root (and that a case could be marked a mixture of both).[59] R. Moris, who studied the social forces behind urban suicide, raises the concern over the difference of these types of suicide, which he sees as consequent to the frustration of the need for social solidarity. (These drives have to be assumed to exist prior to society in the basic sense that they are not the result of socialization.)[60]

On Durkheim's model, the self's nature is composed of a few basic needs; primarily, a representation of a world is required. We are from our particular points of view mirrors of society. We interpret our selves (and our experiences) as forming a narrative that chronicles what we have "been through" (and hope for).

We see a unique strain of Romanticism in Durkheim's thought. Unlike Kierkegaard, he is not necessarily led to an ascetic ethic. He rather conforms to the typical romantic evaluation of the temporal world; it is good. Nor does he wish to base his knowledge of human nature on personal introspection; he wants to be scientific (i.e., obtain results based on statistical studies that yield predictions). Unlike the romantics, however, he emphasizes society over the individual. All he requires, so it seems, is that social integration is sufficient for selfhood. Unlike Kierkegaard, he places the fruition of the self in a social setting, not in relation to God.

Yet, being cognizant of Durkheim's social agenda is important for understanding the commonality between himself and Kierkegaard. Durkheim, recall, restricts social configurations to those who allow a moderate amount of integration (as to avoid the extremes of excessive integration or individualism). For example, he felt concern over how industrial transformation had uprooted man from an otherwise meaningful network of social relations. Unsavoury social settings are taken to be so precisely because they conflict with Durkheim's idea of what a self is. He has, at the very least, like Kierkegaard, a metaphysical conception of the self, and an accompanying social critique.

Durkheim, it is important to note, preferred a social configuration with the qualities that he felt would allow us to come to fruition as full human beings. He was hostile, in theory and practice, to social circumstances that promoted excessive individualism typical of the nineteenth-century industrial world. Though he did not require the abandonment of industrial society (the way some romantics did), he did want to attempt to heal the wounds caused by social transformation, and attempt to fill in the potholes of meaninglessness typical of the new world (and reflected in some of its literature). The romantic dilemma, thus considered, seems to cause a cleavage, to put it bluntly, between being alone (Kierkegaard) and being with others (the sociologists).

As mentioned earlier, Durkheim seems to mark an obvious break with Kierkegaard. We needed to investigate, however, to what extent, if any, Durkheim's account of the self complements Kierkegaard's. In this chapter we saw that Durkheim may help us to fill in and expand Kierkegaard's account. D. W. Winnicott, a counsellor of the maladjusted, allows us to reconcile the dilemma, bringing together Kierkegaard and the sociologists. The next chapter focuses on his perspective.

⁓ 8 ⁓

WINNICOTT

D. W. WINNICOTT, a psychoanalyst, proposes the following three stages of self-development: dependence, independence, and interdependence. On Winnicott's account, the ground of the self is located within the world of social relations. Nevertheless, he contends, "Human nature does not change."[1] I shall argue that his concept of "interdependence" reconciles the romantic's dilemma whether the self finds fulfilment, ultimately, by being alone (with God or nature) or with her fellows (as Durkheim seems to suggest).

I have drawn a connection between Kierkegaard and Rousseau, and suggested that perhaps Durkheim need not be a foe. Yet, so far, I have only hinted that the sociological school may help us revise Kierkegaard's account. We need to see how to bring the two schools together. We will see how Winnicott's concept of interdependence allows us to expand Kierkegaard's account of the self in light of the sociological school. I proceed by considering each of Winnicott's stages.

DEPENDENCE AND INDEPENDENCE

Winnicott was initially interested in Freud's idea that mental illness could be traced to trauma in early childhood.[2] The early years of life are, according to Winnicott, characterized by dependence. Taking Freud as his point of departure, Winnicott surmised that if there were problems with meeting the early needs, these could be repercussions at later stages of development.

The main feature of Winnicott's approach is an emphasis on the environment as a contributing factor to the development of the self. He writes, "Providing for the child is therefore a matter of providing the environment that facilitates individual mental health and emotional development."[3] Winnicott does not think that one can even become a human being without a proper social context. He contends that defining health as an absence of illness is not good enough.[4] Mental health is about becoming a full human being.

Winnicott writes, "But the fact is that life itself is difficult, and psychology concerns itself with the inherent problems of individual development and of the socialization process..."[5] He says, for example, "We look with suspicion on any theory of schizophrenia that divorces the subject from the problems of ordinary living and the universals of individual development in a given environment."[6]

Winnicott provides an example of his approach: "A psycho-analyst comes to the subject of guilt as one who is in the habit of thinking in terms of growth, in terms of the evolution of the human individual, the individual person, and in relation to the environment."[7] That is, he looks to the environment to find the causes of mental aliments. For him, mental illness is a self-defence mechanism, a reaction to an aversive environment. More generally, he says, "Today, I suggest, we are coming round to the view that in psychosis it is a very primitive defence that is brought into play and organized, because of environmental abnormalities."[8]

Upon Winnicott's account of mental illness, schizophrenia, for instance, is viewed as a regression to a more primitive mode of existence. In order to escape present difficulties; we take flight to a more rudimentary self.[9] Winnicott posits the idea that an aversive environment could cause the positing of a fake self (in order to protect the real self).[10] Thus, we may embark on the path of regression because of previous problems encountered in the maturation process (relating to an insufficient environment). Mental illness is often suffered as a consequence of a problem whose etiology is rooted in the human environment of our relations to others.[11] According to Winnicott, it is clear that we can be unwell even in the absence of obvious physical problems.[12]

The point of development is to not remain dependent (like the child). Winnicott points out that the environment facilitates the conditions for the realization of potentials. For instance, the etymology of the word "infant" can be traced back to "not talking." We are born without being able to speak, but are later granted speech by our environment. Similarly, the environment ideally "enables a child to realize potential" in every other field as well.[13]

The infant cannot see itself as separate from its environment (usually the mother). The first stage of development is thus characterized by pure dependence.[14] As Winnicott says, "If dependence really does mean dependence, then the history of an individual baby cannot be written in terms of the baby alone. It must be written in terms also of the environmental provision which either meets dependence needs or fails to meet them."[15] The dependence that is experienced in infancy is mitigated by a move toward greater independence by a transitional object.

The transitional object, according to Winnicott, occupies a space of both imagination and reality. The transitional object takes the place of the mother, and hence shifts the dependence from the mother to the object (be it a toy, pacifier, blanket, or whatever). The child clings to the object, which on the one hand has reality as a real thing in the world, yet on the other is also imaginary insofar as the object substitutes the mother for the child). As we become dependent upon transitional objects, at least in fantasy, and to the extent that these objects are invested with emotional energy—cathected, to use Freudian jargon—we move in the direction of greater independence.

According to Winnicott, it is only when we recognize that we are not the environment that we are said to be self-conscious. A child does not necessarily understand "I am gone to the store." For the child, when the mother is present, she is there, and when she is absent, she is dead. (This is not to suggest the child understands the concept of death but, rather, that the object is absent without the understanding it shall return.)

Winnicott adopts the phrase "going-on-being" to characterize our growth. (He also uses the word "journey.") According to Winnicott, the process of becoming a self involves the past (who we were), the present (who we are), and the future (who we want to be).[16] Within its history, there is a continuity that characterizes the self. Winnicott writes:

> The psyche begins as an imaginative elaboration of physical functioning, having as its most important duty the binding together of past experiences, potentialities, and the present moment awareness, and expectancy for the future. Thus the self comes into existence.[17]

According to Winnicott, creativity is central to human development because it involves how we deal with the future: "the link can be made, and usefully made, between creative living and living itself, and the reasons can be studied why it is that creative living can be lost and why the individual's feeling that life is real or meaningful can disappear."[18] Winnicott, in fact, sometimes uses the idea of not feeling real as a measure of ill health.[19]

Play is also important in human development, because it aids us on the road to independence. It is through play that we can separate ourselves from the moment, make plans, and mentally conceive of different states of affairs. Play, Winnicott contends, occupies a space between reality (e.g., the necessity of social norms) and imagination (where rules may be transgressed).[20] Winnicott notes that becoming lost in either extreme, however, whether imagination or reality, is an illness of sorts.[21]

Winnicott conceives of psychotherapy as a situation in which the therapist becomes the transitional object, invested with emotional energy, only to exercise the movement to autonomy. Whereas Freudian psychotherapy recreates and works out unresolved Oedipal conflicts, Winnicott's brand of psychotherapy plays out a transition to a greater independence than was achieved in childhood. The successful achievement of independence, however, is not where Winnicott ends his story of the self.

INTERDEPENDENCE

According to Winnicott, morality is not external to us—it does not require the mediation of God—but should rather be seen as an innate human capacity.[22] Yet, the acquisition of morality requires a social context in much the same way as the acquisition of independence requires the support of social relations. He writes:

> The dynamic is the growth process, this being inherited by each individual. Taken for granted, here, is the good-enough facilitating environment, which at the start of each individual's growth and development is the *sine qua non*...[23]

If we do not get the support we need, he contends, we are bound to remain dependent as a symptom of the lack of a satisfactory facilitating environment.

Winnicott thinks that it is important to be able to be alone.[24] He writes, "Maturity and the capacity to be alone implies that the individual has had the chance through good-enough mothering to build up a belief in a benign environment. This belief is built up through a repetition of satisfactory instinctual gratifications."[25] As he explains, "The state of being alone is something which (though paradoxically) always implies that someone else is there."[26] We are never alone in the sense that we are part of an entire web of social meanings that we carry with us in our "internal environment." By being well integrated, we can be outwardly independent. Winnicott says:

> Independence is never absolute. The healthy individual does not become isolated, but becomes related to the environment in such a way that the individual and the environment can be said to be interdependent...The value of this approach is that it enables us to study and discuss at one and the same time the personal and the environmental factors. In this language health means both the health of the individual and the health of society, and full maturity of the individual is not possible in an immature or ill social setting.[27]

Winnicott recognizes both the social context and individual as being contributors to the development of a self.[28] He writes:

> Independence does not become absolute, and the individual seen as an autonomous unit is in fact never independent of his environment, though there are ways by which in maturity the individual may FEEL free and independent, as much as makes for happiness and for a sense of having a personal identity.[29]

Winnicott is careful to qualify that having a sense of belonging must depend on an environment with genuine social bonds. Thus, he says, only a real local community can satisfy the needs of social belonging:

> We need to accept the fact that psychiatrically healthy persons depend for their health and for their personal fulfilment on loyalty to a delimited area of society, perhaps the local bowls club. And why not?[30]

In his practice, in fact, he started noticing that his patients complained of feelings of not being real and of feeling separate from the world, which suggest a collective aberration much like that discussed by Durkheim.[31]

Broadly, the theological and sociological accounts are both within the romantic tradition in terms of subjectivity, social critique and teleology.[32] Winnicott's theory, specifically, also bears similar generic resemblances to Kierkegaard's. For both Kierkegaard and Winnicott, there are three stages of development that can be related thus: dependence (the aesthete), independence (the ethical man), and interdependence (the religious). Winnicott furthermore thinks that too much dependence or independence is a sign of mental illness. Similarly, in Kierkegaard's thought, reality is associated with necessity, and imagination with possibility; going to either extreme leads to the despair experienced by the ethical man and the aesthete, respectively.

Winnicott wondered whether the types of mental illness he encountered as a psychotherapist might perhaps have been related to the time in which he lived. It is at least plausible then to assume that he would have been receptive to the sort of social critiques of the industrial age typical of the romantics.

Kierkegaard and the sociologist, however, seemingly part company on whether the self finds fulfilment alone (Kierkegaard) or with others (e.g., Durkheim). Winnicott's psychology offers a solution to this romanticist dilemma with his idea of interdependence. For Winnicott, psychological growth is not complete until one has reached a state of interdependence, with the autonomy of the individual preserved. Winnicott's idea of interdependence captures what the romantics, more generally, intended, that is, a desire to avoid two modern enigmas: alienation (where we are isolated) and totalitarianism (where we are engulfed).

The notion of interdependence is consistent with Kierkegaard's view that we have to be alone with God (separated from our fellows and dependent upon him) in order to have a ground for ethics—independent action that relates to our fellows. Even for Kierkegaard, as I remarked in chapter 3, there is, in the end, a social dimension to the self.

The notion of interdependence is also consistent with Rousseau's and Durkheim's emphasis on the social conditions for autonomy without annulling it. Being in a social context does not annul free choice but, rather, makes it intelligible. What I can choose is of course in part socially determined; free will is to choose from within the set of broadly understood socially assigned possibilities, not to will in a vacuum. For instance, there are things a member of the Zulu tribe could aspire to, for example, some place of status within the organization, that are not even possible for me. The issue of free will is no basis to think there is an unbridgeable chasm between Kierkegaard and say, Durkheim.

In fact, Winnicott's concept of interdependence can reconcile a tension in the history of romantic thought: in the case of Rousseau, for instance, where we are pulled between two competing visions of human fulfilment, that of being alone or with others. Winnicott captures the dynamic nature of the self, and pays heed to social and individualistic aspects, which Kierkegaard, it is plausible to think, would endorse.

For Winnicott, however, it is not God but our fellow human beings who help us become interdependent. (God could well figure in Winnicott's theory as a ruse on which to organize a social group, though.) God, according to Kierkegaard, helps us be independent and relate to others ethically (the man–God–man relationship). Only in the religious stage does man achieve interdependence. Nevertheless, what is noteworthy, for the purposes of my argument, is that the final stage of human development, for both thinkers, can be characterized by interdependence, though the substance differs. Even if we sit alone, engaged in a mathematical, musical, or literary investigation, we are conversing through the social mediums these pursuits provide. Kierkegaard and the sociologists agree, it is plausible to think, that our lives as persons (as opposed to, say, automata), our limitations and aspirations, require a social vehicle. I will not dwell on the God-relationship, since my main objective is to explore what can be gained from bringing the two schools of thought together.

We may wish to notice in passing, however, the following caveats to the notion of interdependence upon which I have put emphasis. First, it is reasonable to assume that interdependence can be frustrated if the necessary prerequisites, such as freedom from extreme forms of oppression, are not obtained. Social injustice must be confronted precisely because it is antithetical to human flourishing. Durkheim details how the self can, for instance, come apart when society goes to extremes of egoism or envelopment. Furthermore, he illustrates the idea that a theory of the self can be a bulwark against social injustices; it can guide public policy. Interestingly, the generically Kierkegaardian theory of the self, developed hitherto, has historically provided the basis for social action, as I shall attempt to illustrate.

Second, as stated in the introduction, it is my intention to develop a Kierkegaardian account of the self, and in the interest of that pursuit I reserve the right, when appropriate, to go beyond what he says. Kierkegaard's theory requires emendation, and justifies a need to go beyond his own writings. His account of the self is rendered robust by explaining the social dimension of the self that seems derivative in his account. Although there is a social element in Kierkegaard's account of the self already (the man–God–man relationship), it can be further developed and emphasized, inspired by Rousseau, Durkheim, and Winnicott. For example, Winnicott's concept of interdependence allows us to view sociological thought as a complement to Kierkegaard's theory of the self.

Next I shall consider some of the possible consequences for practice of adopting the purely theological or sociological conception of the self. I shall also consider results yielded by adopting the generically Kierkegaardian approach, which takes into account the sociological tradition of Rousseau, Durkheim, and Winnicott.

3

SOME CONSEQUENCES
FOR PRACTICE

THE IDEA OF SUICIDE

IN THE PREVIOUS CHAPTER, I argued that there are important commonalities between the theological and sociological conceptions of the self. However, these respective approaches have yielded vastly different consequences for practice. To appreciate the legacy of the Romantic movement with respect to theories of the self, it is important to consider its consequences for practice. I have chosen to focus on the phenomenon of suicide to illustrate how the transition from a theological to a sociological self influenced social practices relating to self-killing.

We are well served by uncovering historical disparities in practice between the theological and sociological schools, before we can hope to bring them together in practice. We shall see that the theological and sociological schools did indeed result in divergent practices. I first show suicide conceived of as a moral problem and, later, as a social one.

MORAL PROBLEM

It was Pliny who, in the first century CE, pointed out that a deity's one flaw is his inability to commit suicide. In all probability, suicide has been familiar, both as thought and deed, to all cultures in all times. In some cases we have records to support this assumption: von Hoff, for instance, catalogues 960 cases of suicide in classical antiquity, by sex, culture, method, motive, accomplishment (was it successful?), reality (was it fictitious?), and source (what is the origin of the information?).[1] He records suicide as the cause of death of numerous philosophers of the ancient world.[2]

In the *Phaedo*, however, Socrates suggests that we do not have the right to kill ourselves because we are God's property (and we should not kill that which does not belong to us). Aristotle viewed suicide as an illegitimate act (an act against the state), while Aquinas saw it as a violation of the natural law (the will to live, which was put there by God). For Augustine suicide was against the sixth commandment (not to kill), as it merely represented a peculiar form of murder, that is, self-murder. Common to all four thinkers—Socrates, Aristotle, Aquinas, and Augustine—was the notion that suicide is rebellion, be it against God, society, nature, or the law.

There was no word that we know of for suicide in ancient Greece; the word *suicide* was, in fact, coined in the seventeenth century and only Caramel the theologian used the neologism, *suicidium*, which was adopted by the Frenchman Abbé Desfontaines in 1737.[3] The overriding concern for the ancients was the ethical status of the act; the virtue or vice of it, whether it was to be considered noble or ignoble. In *Historia Zoon*, Aristotle tells the tale of a mare that killed herself by throwing herself into an abyss for having mated with her offspring. Here we have an Oedipal motif, in which suicide follows incest. It seems to suggest that suicide may be ethically permissible (even encouraged?) when it follows an act that is perceived to violate nature. In the same vein, a woman who killed herself after being raped could have been considered to have acted nobly, since she killed herself out of shame (*pudor*).

The ancient world saw suicide from a strictly moral perspective in that certain situations did not just excuse the act but almost called for it as the only possible response if one were to retain or regain one's dignity. Women killing themselves to avoid assault by conquerors, or even a woman killing herself if not able to "fulfill herself as a woman" through the institution of marriage, are examples cited of situations in which suicide could be considered a noble act.

Furthermore, certain methods of suicide were considered more noble than others, such as starving oneself (*in edia*), or throwing oneself upon a sword. The former act is in the tradition of the philosopher, and the latter has a soldierly connotation. If honour was at stake, the statesman or soldier could be said to have a duty to commit suicide. In a militaristic state, for instance, where regimentation and conformity are valued, suicide is the ultimate expression of obedience to society. In Rome, for example, death by suicide was a matter of honour for the soldier or slave.[4] Suicide by hanging or jumping was, however, considered ignoble and vulgar in that it conveyed desperation and injured the integrity of the body.

The legality of various forms of suicide became a matter of some judicial wrangling.[5] A taxonomy of different reasons for the act formed a virtual discipline of suicide, where some, such as weariness or hatred of life, were considered acceptable means for the act. There were, in fact, numerous ways of indicating cause of death by suicide (which allowed legal appraisal). Suicide could be caused by madness (*mania*), nobility of the soul (*eupsychia*), despair (*desperatta salus, desperatio*), loyalty (*fides*), grief (*dolor*), guilt (*mala conscientia*), despondency (*athymaia*), weariness of life (*taedium vitae*), insufferable pain (*impatientia doloris*), shame (*pudor*), anger (*ira*), frenzy (*furor*), fit of insanity (*mente torbata*), ostentation (*iactatio*), or being ordered to carry out the act (*necessitas*).

In the Middle Ages, suicide was mostly represented as an act of despair (*desperatio*). Despair was the central category in assessing suicide. Despair was a sin, a renunciation of God, hope, and faith (as in the case of Judas).[6] Since God extends the promise of salvation, a suicide is rebellion against grace. Kierkegaard also saw suicide as a permanent sin: an abandonment of one's task to become oneself. The Christian ethics around suicide were developed around 400 CE; Ambrose and Augustine struggled to justify self-killing in the case of women seeking to avoid violation (and it was Augustine who would set the tone for the moral views and canonical laws of the church).[7]

In England, the council of Hertford had adopted a canon in 672 CE denying suicides a normal burial (although one thousand madmen had been exempted). In the sixteenth century, self-murder was still considered a serious crime and was often punished.[8] Suicide was viewed as a moral failing, a case of having been "tempted by the devil." Some thought suicides ended up wandering the world as estranged ghosts, forever condemned from the world of the living and unlikely to gain entry into heaven. Perhaps an attempt at stopping these ghostly wanderings lay behind the popular custom of burying the suicide at a crossroads with a stake driven through his chest. Given the moral attitudes surrounding suicide, well-to-do suicides often ended up being ruled "accidental deaths," so as not to defile the status of the person and family.

Attitudes to suicide did not change much over the centuries. To be charged with death by suicide in Victorian England could entail posthumous punishments, such as being denied a church burial and having life insurance declared null and void. Family disgrace often ensued. Up until 1882, a suicide had to be buried privately by the police upon orders of the coroner (between the hours of nine and twelve at night).[9]

Punishing a suicide was of course not a simple matter, as the person guilty of the crime was dead. Punishing members of the suicide's family was a considered option, a practice Voltaire criticized, but this was in many ways unsatisfactory and the problematic remained. An attempted suicide, on the other hand, did not present the same awkward dilemma as that person was alive to receive his or her punishment.

In the nineteenth century, suicide was still seen as a sin, a cowardly act. The nineteenth century periodicals, for instance, sometimes blamed the increasing safety of daily life for a reduction in courage and manliness, which was thought to result in suicide.[10] In fact, in England, the Army Act of 1881 made suicide a military offence.[11]

SOCIAL PROBLEM

Thomas G. Masaryk put forward the thesis in 1878 that suicide is a symptom of modern civilization, the most notable feature of which is the decline of religion; he also held that suicide was not present in primitive societies.[12] He claimed that suicide was a "mass phenomenon" particular to modern culture[13] and hoped he could locate the "sickness of our century."[14] According to him, a mentally healthy person is in harmony with the environment (or at least has a perception of how things ought to be).[15] Basically, Masaryk paints the old dilemma between civilization and nature, typical of romantic thought such as Rousseau's. Civilization, or at least aspects of it, leads to illness, whereas nature, or a more primitive existence, represents freedom.[16] His basic assumptions are that suicide represents the fruition of a long process, which is rooted in a historical process of a society.[17] He writes:

> In the Middle Ages there were probably few mentally ill and no general widespread nervousness; only in the present era does mental illness and its corresponding psychosis generally increase...[suicide is] the most significant sign of our times.[18]

The march of technological progress has a dark side: social disintegration. Since Durkheim wrote and published his famous investigation into the etiology of suicide, sociologists have busied themselves carrying out an extension of his legacy.[19] In the tradition of Durkheim, they have tended to use social integration as the central factor in explaining social ills. Integration is understood as the accord between the individual's needs, aspirations, attitudes, and values and those of his group.[20] If we share a common outlook with the rest of our community, we could be said to be well integrated. Yet, if we are radically at odds with the community in which we exist, we may be alienated (which is a factor in suicide rates, according to Durkheim).[21]

As early as 1852, Henry Buckle published a book drawing on suicide statistics, which provided prima materia for the positivistic approach to society (and hence suicide). Suicide was to be prevented as a symptom of a social ill within the body politic. Suicide, if it was an evil, was a social one. For some, suicide was to be the gauge of the effects of social change.

Yet, the number of deaths registered as suicides may be skewed; the methods of acquisition, and class of those categorized, render these statistics fallible. For instance, since there is (still) a stigma attached to suicide, many may be classified as "accidents." In early modern England, for example, a coroner would get news of a sudden death from private individuals, doctors, policemen, institutions such as asylums and hospitals, or from the registrar of death. Most of these proved to be unreliable sources as they had interests of their own to protect: family members were reluctant to admit to the shame of a suicide in their midst, doctors were trying to avoid a bad reputation, while the police were not under regulations requiring reporting of sudden death. The registrar only had to report sudden death under certain conditions. In such cases as women "found drowned," it was easy to report an accidental drowning.

In spite of unreliable data the move was on to explain suicide from a scientific point of view. The positivistic approach of finding the cause of suicide led to a preoccupation with geography in an effort to discern patterns, such as why suicide rates appeared to be higher in certain areas than others. The approach of discerning patterns based on geography was applied to bastardy, drunkenness, and cholera, before it was first tried with regards to suicide in 1859.[22] From preliminary studies it was concluded that the etiology lay in vicious or morbid tones of thought (Radcliffe 1862). In about 1880, Morselli related suicide to climate and landscape, stating that it was lower in mountainous regions and areas with extreme climates and higher in flat and fertile areas with rivers.

In 1930, Durkheim's pupil Maurice Halbwachs expanded on this geographical perspective, saying that land terrain influenced occupation, which in turn influenced the suicide rate. The new approach, then, was to compare occupations (agricultural-rural/industrial-urban) with suicide rates. Suicide, together with other social ills such as sexual repression and violent crime were seen as inevitable consequences of the progress of "civilization." Twentieth-century sociologists traced the thought prints of eighteenth-century romantics in viewing these phenomena as significant of the move away from nature.

Social scientists sought to uncover the truth of suicide, which helped shift the focus on suicide away from the moral dimension and toward a scientific-medical assessment. As a social phenomenon suicide required explanation, and the adoption of scientific methodology engendered hope of revealing the causes of suicide. The view adopted of suicide was one of a health problem, an aberration, which needed to be dealt with by a host of experts: psychiatrists, sociologists, social workers, and an entire apparatus of the medical-science community, which gave birth to a new discipline, namely suicidology.[23]

I have not attempted to show we ought to view, or deal with, individual suicides. I have pointed out, however, that suicide moved from the governance of the (Christian) ethical-religious regime of power during the Middle Ages to becoming the focus of a medical-scientific community and of an entire apparatus of experts in the production of new knowledge. As far as suicide continued to pose a problem, it was a social one, which required an uncovering of the truth behind it.

We can bring the theological and sociological accounts together in practice without being blind to how they can, and have, diverged. In this chapter, we saw that the theological and sociological schools resulted in divergent practices related to suicide.

In the next chapter, I take a look at schizophrenia, with the aim of examining in more detail what is at stake for practice in adopting a specific theory of the self.

⟡ 10 ⟡

SUICIDE AND SCHIZOPHRENIA

FROM THE EIGHTEENTH CENTURY ONWARD, schizophrenia, like suicide, has been presented as a phenomenon needing scientific explanation. Schizophrenia was to psychologists what suicide was for sociologists. I shall further probe the effects upon practice in dealing with suicide and, then, schizophrenia, by adopting one of three approaches: physiological, sociological, or psychological.

To understand what is at stake in adopting a Kierkegaardian conception of the self requires considering something other than suicide. In this chapter, in addition to suicide, we will consider schizophrenia from a variety of different perspectives.

I shall begin by adopting the same physiological approach hereto, in order to link the following to the theological and sociological accounts of earlier chapters. (The theological and sociological approaches often share a uniform approach to practice.) Also, please bear in mind that, for the purpose of this study, the sociological and psychological approaches should be viewed as variants on the same theme; that is, the self is comprehended within a social network, be that societal (as it is, primarily, for the sociologist), or, for example, in the family context (as it is, primarily, for the psychologist). I shall discuss both approaches toward the end of this chapter.

SUICIDE: THREE APPROACHES
D. Lester, in a study of the biochemical basis of suicide, has pointed out that different models exist to explain abnormal behaviour (such as suicide). Sociological explanations offer a particular societal situation as the cause of suicide. A behaviourist explanation claims suicide to be learned behaviour. A psychological view contends that the cause of suicide can always be traced to the mind. In medicine, suicidal behaviour is analysed from a physiological standpoint.[1] Lester says:

> The medical model takes disease as the basis for discussing abnormal behaviour. Let us say you have cancer. The physician will ask you what **symptoms** you have. He may perform certain tests to gather more information about your state. He finally decides upon a **diagnosis**, that

is, what particular **illness** it is that you are suffering from. He then may
send you off to a **hospital**, where you will become a **patient** and receive
therapy until you are **cured** and released.[2]

Research into the neurological sources of depression led to investigations
of a physiological cause of suicide. Seeing that most suicides are committed
as a consequence of profound depression, this linking was natural. If we can
explain the physiological basis for depression, we can do the same, so the
thinking goes, for suicide.[3] For instance:

> Since corn has low levels of tryptophan as compared to other cereals,
> Mawson and Jacobs (1978) argued that people who eat corn in preference
> to other cereals would have a lesser intake of tryptophan. They
> hypothesized, therefore, that nations with a higher per capita consumption
> of corn would have a higher homicide rate. A study of nations in 1972
> confirmed this hypothesis. Lester (1985) replicated this study for the year
> of 1978 and included suicide rates. Lester found no association for the
> sample of 38 nations between per capita corn consumption and either
> suicide or homicide rates.[4]

Yet the medical model often does not hold when we apply it to mental distress.
In some psychiatric diagnoses, symptoms are grouped together under a new
word sign. Rather than classing conditions based on their root causes, they are
thus classified by similarity of symptoms.

When psychological symptoms are traced to physiological conditions,
however, an epistemological ambiguity remains (which is not the case with
physical ailments). For example, when we are in fear, we exhibit heightened
levels of adrenaline in our blood. However, deducing from this that the presence
of adrenaline was the cause of our fear—rather than, say, the man with a knife
chasing us—would be wrong. Studies of the etiology of mental illness are often
not conclusive as to whether physiological aberrations caused the symptoms
(or the social context caused the aberrations, which caused the symptoms).
For example:

> Bunney and Fawett felt that suicidal action takes place when the individual
> is suffering unbearably, and so it is not surprising that this is reflected in
> biochemical changes in the body that are sensitive to stress.[5]

Since both physiological changes and psychological ones may be present, it is
difficult to isolate the etiological cause (of abnormal behaviour).

The danger lies in thinking that only one approach can explain suicide.
Durkheim's thesis that suicide rates vary inversely with social integration, for
instance, was to usurp psychological as well as other types of explanations.
He avoided factors such as gender and race because of the possibility of thus
introducing biological factors, and has subsequently been reprimanded for
this decision.

It has been suggested that if he had admitted that there can be, for instance, psychological causes of suicide, he could have accounted for anomalies in his research (that is, suicides when social integration is present).[6] Exponents of the sociological model of explanation for suicide have tried to make their view more plausible by denying that they can explain specific suicides (only suicide rates in general). It has become increasingly obvious, since Durkheim's seminal work, however, that no type of explanation, be it biological, sociological, or psychological, can adequately explain human phenomena to the exclusion of others.[7] Lester, for example, suggests that some models might better explain certain cases than others. He suggests that rather than viewing the theories as competing, we should consider the possibility that they may all contribute to our understanding of mental illness. I now turn to approaches to suicide upon the adoption of a generically psychological conception of the self, thereby expanding the argument.

The psychological approach locates the cause of suicide as consequent to certain mental states (which may be deemed pathological). Some have proclaimed, for instance, that "suicide is a remedy to intolerable situation-existence," or is the result of "no hope."[8] Baechler, in his study of suicides, claims that it occurs when people can no longer live and maintain their self-image; he essentially views suicide as a positive act used to resolve an existential problem.[9] Sociologists, not surprisingly, have accused the psychological practitioners of being overly individualistic.

Yet, what bound the sociological and psychological theorist together was a belief that what they were doing had repercussions for justice. They wished to, each in their own way, correct the imposition of technological society upon the individual (often, ironically, with their own technologies). J. Hillman's book, *We've Had One Hundred Years of Psychoanalysis and the World is Worse*, is designed to prompt the following reaction. We have a litany of specialists—sociologists, suicidologists, psychiatrists, social workers, and social engineers—in spite of which we do not appear to be in better shape.

Hillman says, "Whatever treatment directly neglects experience as such and hastens to reduce or overcome it, something is being done against the soul. For experience is the soul's one and only nourishment."[10] Hillman is perhaps one of the most radical heretics of modern medical psychiatry. He says, for example, that he is interested in suicide prevention in relation to "death and the soul."[11] With the case of suicide, Hillman thinks that the goal of the analyst is to confirm the experiences of the person (and not deny, lay blame, or prevent). Suicide asserts the independent reality of the soul; and perhaps nothing makes us more cognizant of our soul (or another's) than death.

Hillman recognizes that his views are antithetical to the medical establishment, for as he sees it the root metaphor of all scientific medicine rests on a "dread of death."[12] According to Hillman, if suicide or depression is necessary for a person, it may take a metaphoric death before renewal can occur (although a "metaphoric death" can of course lead to an actual suicide). According to Hillman, it is despair that opens the door to the experience of death, and that offers a chance for transformation.[13]

Hillman's anti-scientism places him squarely in the romantic tradition. His approach acknowledges the limits of theorizing on such matters. He asserts, for instance, that whatever we think about the soul will be both right and wrong, if it hits the mark at all.[14] The individual soul, according to him, is such that only when we speak as to court contradiction can we approach its truth.

Consider the words of two adolescents:

> The whole time I was in the first hospital nobody tried to deal with my problems. They just tried to subdue me with pills. I saw a psychiatrist once a week and it wasn't even for an hour. He'd only pop in and wave. Sometimes he'd speak to you. But he never really spoke to you. He'd just tell you what they were going to do to you next.[15]

> He didn't realize the state of my depression. He just put me on anti-depressant pills and let me go back to what was happening.[16]

Rubkin, who examined adolescent suicide at some length, wrote a book that was not intended as a contribution to science but as a human expression of the act (of suicide).[17] She concludes, "With the extended family shattered and with the nuclear family possibly deteriorating, they have little sense of belonging, of tradition, and of the role they will play in society."[18]

SCHIZOPHRENIA: THREE APPROACHES

The word "schizophrenia" originates from the Greek, and is composed of two basic parts: *schizein* meaning "to cleave," and *phren* meaning "mind." The etymology points toward understanding the term as "divided mind." The term "schizophrenia" was first coined by Eugen Bleuer, and took the place of the older term *dementia praecox*. The new term was to replace an older one that had moral associations (which the new scientific one was not supposed to have). In fact, the changes in terms were a key move in legitimizing "mental illness" as a medical ailment (which arose with the attempt to make psychology into a science).

Psychiatrists categorize a multitude of symptoms under the umbrella term "schizophrenia." Roman and Trice, who conducted studies of schizophrenia in relation to poverty, found five essential traits that combine to make up the character of schizophrenia. The most basic characteristic of schizophrenia, they claim, is a disturbance in relationships with other people and the environment in general.[19] Second, the symptoms are manifest episodically and not continuously. Third, it is "a syndrome marked by spontaneous breaks in reality relationships in such a way that the individual is unable to perceive the meaning of objects and symbols in his environment in relation to his own needs, goals, and experiences."[20] Fourth, there is a marked fragmentation and peculiarity of thought and speech patterns. Fifth, there is evidence of personality and identity disintegration. The authors of the above characterization, however, go on to note that it is of limited use to define schizophrenia by symptoms alone, as they will differ in individual cases. While one person demonstrates the above features in a particular configuration, another may show a different propensity toward these same characteristics.

Roman and Trice also attempt to identify characteristics of the schizophrenic's personal history. They propose that, generally, the familial situation of many schizophrenics appears to be characterized by (1) over-protection and, at the same time, (2) rejection. The family of many schizophrenics are marked by rigidity, and a general lack of flexibility.

Schizophrenic behaviour has been interpreted in various ways throughout history: in the seventeenth century it was often viewed as a result of being bewitched or controlled by demons; in later times, the control over the individual has been thought to originate in the effects of electricity, telepathy, television, or the government. The underling theme, however, remains the same: the schizophrenic's sensation of having his thoughts and/or behaviour controlled by something or someone outside himself.[21]

L. Jacobs, who studies the social context of schizophrenia, also considers the biological basis for the condition:

> Schizophrenia is essentially an extreme human response to environmental stress pertaining to relating to other human beings, and occurs in persons with a special vulnerability, which is either genetic or acquired during childhood.[22]

He goes on to say:

> Since it is not possible to base a meaningful biological study on the diagnostic systems employed at present in psychiatry, the word schizophrenia will be used in this treatise to refer to any disorder characterized by a chronic, usually debilitating psychotic state, most frequently arising between the ages of fifteen and forty-five and generally of a progressive nature, although often intermittent.[23]

Furthermore, Jacobs claims that the creative seem to have a tendency toward schizophrenia: "Schizophrenia can then be looked upon as the price which the human race must pay for its superior members."[24]

Karlsson writes, "The evidence does not support the view that a faulty environment is responsible for the origin of schizophrenia, but rather stress seems to bring out or aggravate the symptoms in persons with a schizophrenic constitution."[25] He gives a privileged position to physiological explanation as he thinks we are born with a certain "constitution." However, Karlsson also writes:

> The times are past in which geneticists felt that the recognition biological determinants of the mind constitutes a denial of its flexibility under social and cultural influences. Just as no biological process is known on which genes do not impinge, so no biological process is likely to exist which is not subject to non-genetic variability.[26]

The idea is to say that schizophrenia is caused by a certain physical state may be a necessary condition but not a sufficient one.

Yet, upon the medical model, many times the patient's experiences are re-interpreted from the perspective of the professionals. Consider this statement by a psychiatrist:

> Still other patients are concerned that their words will be recorded, used against them, and spread out on television or in some public display. This is a reflection of the patient's egocentricity, megalomania, exhibitionism, and distrust.[27]

Distrust of the psychiatrist, and the patient's therapy, become further evidence of his "illness"; the psychiatrist's interpretation of the patient seems to ignore the patient's experience, which could have included involuntary sedation, restraint, seclusion, testing (and other acts, that could make one "paranoid").

Diagnoses are often based on tests, which may include the Wechsler-Bellevue Intelligence scale, the Rorschach test, and other projective techniques, such as figure drawings; in addition, each person is graded on an IQ test (full scale, verbal, prorated performance scale), information, comprehension, arithmetic, similarities, digit span, digit symbol, picture completion, block design, and picture arrangement tests. On the basis of these tests, psychiatrists have claimed to be able to make the following diagnoses:

> The tests indicate a patient in grossly psychotic.[28]

> The tests reflect a grossly psychotic paranoid schizophrenic state.[29]

> The tests display a severe chronic schizophrenic psychosis.[30]

> The tests suggests a unsystematized paranoid schizophrenia.[31]

> The tests are consistent with a clinical picture of an acute schizophrenic episode in partial remission.[32]

The approach is based on a medical model, through which psychiatrists attempt to uncover a "disease."[33] P. Barham, another critic of reductive approaches, remarks:

> They certainly intended a scientific undertaking with a powerful predictive capacity that was consonant both with a particular set of scientific aspirations and with a particular from of social experience, with a view of schizophrenic "uselessness" and all that we have seen conveyed by the term "deterioration."[34]

Yet, Barham writes, "A schizophrenic breakdown can only be determined by getting at the meaning that the factors have for the potential schizophrenic."[35]

As the notion of schizophrenia changed, different aspects became more or less emphasized as central to its identification.[36] At the end of the nineteenth century, for example, there was the identification of the chronic schizophrenic.[37] Once one had schizophrenia, it would not go away. The effect of being labelled "mentally ill" and, in addition, "chronic," has a twofold effect. If a medical professional tells us we are "ill," we may start to accept ourselves as so. Further, to be told we have a "chronic" disease does not offer much hope to the individual struggling to gain control of his or her life. Labelling also results in social stigma. Psychiatrists have tended to ignore the psychosocial aspect of illness and just deal with the physiological qualifies, according to some patients, who feel consequently demoralized, as they are discouraged from living without drugs to "get back on their feet."[38] As Shulz and Kilgalen, who studied different cases of schizophrenia, have remarked, "[A] philosophy of hopelessness generates chronicity."[39]

Schizophrenic behaviour, like suicide, may be consequent to a host of factors, physiological, social, familial, and psychological. For example, just as it is sometimes maintained that social disintegration leads to increased suicide rates, it too could be said to contribute to increased rates of mental illness. There are, however, also epistemological problems for the sociological approach. For instance, we have already witnessed that there is considerable dissension on defining what constitutes a mental illness such as schizophrenia. If we were to attempt to measure the rates of schizophrenia, it is obvious that varying definitions would yield different rates, and this would make it hard to demonstrate any correlation between the "disease" and the social situation in which it occurs.[40]

Karlsson thinks, for example, that the diagnosis of schizophrenia into different "types" is "artificial," as different psychiatrists will provide different diagnoses for the same patient, and the terms applied vary among countries. He furthermore claims that the distinction made between "schizophrenia" and "manic depressive psychosis" gives the impression it is arbitrary.[41]

T. Szasz builds on the Karlsson's concern. He published an indictment of modern psychiatry in *The Myth of Mental Illness*. The Commissioner of New York State Department of Mental Hygiene demanded Szasz be dismissed from his university position because he did not "believe in" mental illness.

Szasz says that illness usually has two facets:

> The term "illness" thus refers, first, to an abnormal biological condition whose existence may be claimed, truly or falsely, by patient, physician, and others; and second, to the social role of patient, which may be assumed or assigned.[42]

In the mid-nineteenth century, however, the idea that we could be "sick" without having a physical illness gained currency. Charcot and Freud made mental illness a respectable designation by developing new assignments of symbols, such as malingering (pretending to be sick while not having a physical ailment, the famous case being hysteria). The new language changed "spells" to "seizures" and "quacks" to "psychotherapists," says Szasz.[43]

Szasz recognizes that some people do suffer mentally, but suggests that these people are not ill (as this is not possible based on his definition of illness) but merely have life problems. According to him, rather than try to treat the so-called mentally ill as if they had a disease, we should deal with them as people seeking counselling in an ethical sense.[44] Szasz draws out the consequence for his approach:

> It is common to define psychiatry as a medical speciality concerned with the study, diagnosis, and treatment of mental illness. This is a worthless and misleading definition. Mental illness is a myth. Psychiatrists are not concerned with mental illness and their treatments. In actual practice they deal with personal, social, and ethical problems with living.[45]

Hillman and Szasz have attempted to reconfigure the meaning of therapy in ethical, as opposed to positivistic, terms and are thus in the romantic tradition. They deal with helping us find a way to live. They follow Kierkegaard. Hillman's orientation toward depression, for instance, reflects Kierkegaard's notion that a crisis may be necessary for development. According to Kierkegaard, it is the crisis of despair that propels one onward. More specifically, by taking into account the subjectivity of the suffering person in relation to the social context, they operate with a conception of the self consistent with the Kierkegaardian one developed.

The problems that arose with the defining of schizophrenia, and *dementia praecox* before it, have not been completely put to rest. We are perhaps forced to examine Kierkegaard or philosophy more generally.

To understand what is at stake in adopting a Kierkegaardian conception of the self requires considering alternatives. In this chapter, we considered schizophrenia from a variety of different perspectives. In the next chapter, I shall consider the writings of some existential psychiatrists in order to examine in greater detail the repercussions for practice of adopting a generically Kierkegaardian conception of the self.

~ 11 ~

EXISTENTIAL PSYCHOLOGY

AT THE END OF CHAPTER 8, I pointed out that the theological and sociological accounts of the self have commonalities that allow me to categorize them as being generically Kierkegaardian when considering their recent consequences for practice. Though, of course, both approaches would have diverse consequences if held that we can only be fulfilled by a relationship to God. Now turning to the work of Adler, Binswanger, May, and Laing, I contend that their attention to subjectivity, to a social context, together with their conception of human nature, point to the fact that they are practising in a Kierkegaardian tradition.

Attention to subjectivity means taking the patient's point of view under serious and careful consideration, and not unnecessarily reinterpreting the patient's words to fit within a particular terminology or pathology, especially when that would entail reductionism. Attention to social context indicates the belief that all socio-political and historical forces influence an individual's mental state. Finally, adopting an account of human nature means having some notion of what one is meant to be.

I have suggested that it is both possible and desirable to apply a generically Kierkegaardian theory of the self to practice. Since a Kierkegaardian theory has already been employed, in various guises, we need to review the results. We shall consider several key existential psychiatrists who rely on Kierkegaard's theory of self in practice.

I shall first offer brief descriptions of Adler's, Binswanger's, May's, and Laing's respective programs before demonstrating, upon the points under consideration, how they exemplify the Kierkegaardian approach. I shall, finally, attempt to demonstrate the historical relevance of a key Kierkegaardian theme, that of belonging, by considering some remarks by Sartre, who was influencial in popularizing existentialism.

ALFRED ADLER AND LUDWIG BINSWANGER

According to Adler, "The best knower of the human soul will be the one who has lived through passions himself."[1] Presumably observing himself, he infers, "No human being ever appeared except in a community of human beings."[2] Adler goes on:

This social feeling remains throughout life, changed, coloured, circumscribed in some cases, enlarged and broadened in others until it touches not only the members of his own family but also his clan, his nation, and finally the whole of humanity. It is possible that it may exist beyond these boundaries and express itself towards animals, plants, lifeless objects, or finally toward the whole cosmos.[3]

He says, "In order to know how a man thinks, we have to examine his relationship to his fellow man."[4] He points out, for example, that if we have a bodily deformity, we will be treated differently (and this may affect how we see ourselves, as well as how others see us).[5] Adler writes:

We can understand the personality of the individual only when we see him in context, and judge him in his particular situation in the world. By situation we mean place in the cosmos, and his attitude toward his environment and the problems of life, such as the challenges of occupation, contact, and union with his fellow men, which are inherent in his being.[6]

According to Adler, the psyche is teleological (goal-directed).[7] On the one hand, he contends, there is a drive to conformity. On the other hand, there is a drive for superiority, where we want to raise ourselves above others (and to this extent become anti-social).[8] Yet, for Adler, mental health lies in being well integrated with one's fellows.[9] As he says, "Only that individual can go through life without anxiety who is conscious of belonging to the fellowship of man."[10] Adler's idea of what constitutes psychological health is to feel that we belong in a community.

Freud is the point of departure for dynamic psychiatry like Adler's. Binswanger, however, remains critical of Freud and his reductive tendencies. Binswanger's probably greatest dissatisfaction with Freud has to do with Freud's view of religion as an infantile craving to be overcome. Binswanger, conversely, is apt to see religion as an integrated part of what it means to be a human being. He does not try to explain away religion.

Binswanger worries that scientific psychiatry will turn man into an object. (In fact, he claims that a good psychiatrist knows he can never grasp the whole of man with the methods of science.)[11] If we approached one another subjectively, we would have a greater chance, through empathy, he contends, of understanding what it is "like" to be in that person's shoes.

ROLLO MAY
May is, like Binswanger, phenomenological, in the sense of attempting to confront what is given on the surface. His approach begins by seeing a person as something other than merely a "set of diagnostic categories."[12] He writes, "If we are to study and understand man, we need a human model. That sounds like a truism, and it ought to be one; the amazing thing is that it is not a truism at all."[13] Here is an example of how May thinks we should view the mentally ill:

I propose, rather, that the source of this illness was that man had lost his world. The great change that had occurred was the loss of communication with this world, with others, and with him. That is to say, the myths, and symbols had broken down. And the human being, as Epictetus was later to phrase it, "does not know where in the world he is."[14]

According to May anxiety serves a function in a given situation.[15] However, if experienced in a non-specific way, it can lead to a shrinking of our world, dissolution of the self, a blurring of reality, and an inability to properly interpret stimuli. The loss of world entails a loss of self. The goal of psychotherapy, says May, is not to wipe out guilt and anxiety, for example, but to enable us to deal with it constructively.[16]

His emphasis, however, is not on understanding the immediate situation of an individual, but on the situation in which we find ourselves as a society. As May puts it, "The schizoid man is the natural product of technological man."[17] He is apt to speak of an "age of anxiety,"[18] and a sense of the homelessness of modern persons.[19] He says, "It seems more logical to regard rising divorce, suicide, and mental disease rates as symptoms and products of the traumatic transitions of our culture, and to regard anxiety also as a symptom and product of that transitional state."[20] He writes, "I here propose that the quality of anxiety prevalent in the present period arises from the fact that the values and standards underlying modern culture are themselves threatened."[21]

The experience of emptiness, for example, he traces back to a feeling of powerlessness. He writes, "The experience of emptiness, rather, generally comes from people's feeling that they are powerless to do anything effective about their lives or the world they live in."[22] May says, "The experience of emptiness comes when people feel powerless to effect change."[23] The effect of emptiness is not a state in which we can persist for long:

> The human being cannot live in a condition of emptiness for very long: if he is not growing toward something, he does not merely stagnate; the pent-up potentialities turn into morbidity and despair, and eventually into destructive activities.[24]

May remarks, "The chief problem of people in the middle of the twentieth century is emptiness."[25] Although May admits that the feeling of emptiness is not specific to the modern age, he does think the problem has been amplified in modernity. May adds, "Another characteristic of modern people is loneliness. They [modern people] describe this feeling as one of being 'on the outside', isolated, or, if they are sophisticated, they say that they feel alienated."[26] May contends that we must find a cure for our ailments by forging a new way (rather than by looking to a "past that does not exist").[27] He advocates a socio-political program (or at least finding such a program).

R. D. Laing

R. D. Laing contends that mental illness "cannot be grasped through the methods of clinical psychiatry and psycho-pathology as they stand today but, on the contrary, require the existential-phenomenological method to demonstrate their true human relevance and significance."[28]

According to Laing, if we look upon ourselves as objects, we have already strayed into the abstraction where individuals live in isolation; we have already denied our experience of being-in-the-world, our relatedness and interdependence. Laing, therefore, says, "To look and to listen to a patient and to see signs of schizophrenia (as a disease) and to look and to listen to him simply as a human being are to see and to hear in...radically different ways."[29] We must realize that "the ground of the being of all beings is the relation between them."[30] It is subjectivity that allows us to empathize with others.[31] Laing writes, "The main agent in uniting the patient, in allowing the pieces to come together and cohere, is the physician's love, a love that recognizes the patient's total being, and accepts it, with no strings attached."[32] The existential psychologist does not "regard persons as only separate objects in space, who can be studied as any other natural objects can be studied...One will never find persons by studying persons as though they were objects..."[33]

The schizophrenic may claim, for example, to be dead, or Napoleon. Laing explains:

> An exile from the scene of being as we know it, he is an alien, a stranger, signalling to us from the void in which he is foundering, a void which may be peopled by presences that we do not even dream of. They used to be called demons and spirits, and they used to be known and named. He has lost his sense of self, his feelings, his place in the world as we know it. He tells us he is dead.[34]

We should try, Laing implores, to understand the experience world of the schizophrenic. The schizophrenic is what Laing calls ontologically insecure and does not feel a sense of belonging in the world. As Laing points out, "Our behaviour is the function of our experience. We act according to the way we see things."[35]

According to Laing, people generally tend to react to ontological insecurity in two ways. There is a movement toward social acting or isolation. Laing, in fact, discusses four ways in which we try to "save ourselves" from ontological insecurity. The first two cases involve social acting. We may react to our situation through engulfment, by attempting to lose ourselves in a relationship with a person or group. Alternatively, we may react to ontological insecurity through petrification and/or depersonalization, by attempting to confirm our own value by degrading others. The other two ways of dealing with ontological insecurity involve varying degrees of withdrawal. We may react by isolating ourselves; since each glance of the other "threatens one with non-being, with annihilation," others are avoided. Or we may end up suffering the loss of self.

According to Laing, in the process of trying to flee from ourselves (and our situation), we can become unembodied. The schizoid is so self-conscious that all mental processes are observed and spontaneity is lost. He remarks, "The individual has now a persecuting observer in the very core of his being."[36] The techniques of social acting and isolation are, of course, all normal ways we react to various situations in daily life.

That which functioned as a defence from an adverse state of affairs can, in some cases, became a substitution for reality. We go, in common parlance, mad. We take flight into fantasy, where we are omnipotent.[37] Yet, the more we live in fantasy alone, the weaker we become in reality. For instance, sometimes a false self is constructed as a shield against perceived threats. This false self-system can adapt to new environments, and can therefore give the impression of living a normal life till it "cracks."[38] Often those close to those who go mad are surprised when the breakdown into madness occurs.

We can take an example of the process leading to mental illness from Laing's *Sanity, Madness and the Family*. A girl is admitted to a mental hospital in a catatonic state, claiming to be dead and that her mother is trying to kill her. She is diagnosed as being psychotic and suffering from delusions.[39] Yet, according to Laing, these delusions could be intelligible if we reconstruct her world. Existentially, she is dead: she feels that she has no self; she is nobody. In her imaginary world, her negative feelings toward her mother are translated into the delusion that her mother is trying to poison her.

In Laing's research, psychosis is made intelligible "in light of praxis and process of...the family nexus."[40] He says:

> In over 100 cases where we have studied the actual circumstances around the social event when one person comes to be regarded as schizophrenic, it seems to us that without exception the experience and behaviour that gets labelled as schizophrenic is a special strategy that a person invents in order to live in an unliveable situation. In his life situation the person has come to feel he is in an untenable position. He cannot make a move, or make no move, pressures and demands, pushes and pulls, both internally, from himself, and externally, from those around him. He is, as it were, in a position of checkmate.[41]

According to Laing, when threatened by ontological insecurity, we try to flee from ourselves into engulfment, isolation, and implosion.[42] The extreme way to be free from oneself (and one's situation), of course, is suicide. In Psalms, we find the following:

> For my days have become consumed in smoke, And my bones have been scorched like a hearth. My heart has been smitten like grass and withered away, Indeed, I forget to eat my bread, Because of the loudness of my groaning. My bones cling to my flesh. I resemble a pelican in the wilderness; I have become like an owl of the waste places. I lie awake. I have become like a lonely bird on a house-top...My days are like a lengthened shadow; And I wither away like grass.[43]

Also, Nietzsche's words, aimed at modernity, express a disintegration of the self-world nexus:

Whither are we moving now? Away from all suns? Are we not plunging continually? Backward, sideward, forward, in all directions? Is there any up or down left? Are we not straying as through an infinite nothing? Do we not feel the breath of empty space? Has it not become colder? Is not night and more night coming all the while?[44]

COMPARISONS

Henri F. Ellenberger, who wrote a comprehensive history of dynamic psychiatry, notes its relation to older ways of approaching disruptions of the mind. Ellenberger mentions the "soul cures" of tribal societies:

> When a human being has "lost his soul", the shaman works himself into ecstasy by means of a special technique; while he remains in that state, his soul travels to the world of the spirits. Shamans contend to be able, for instance, to track down the lost souls, propitiate them and bring them gifts. Sometimes they have to fight the spirits, preferably with the help of other spirits who are on their side. Even if they are successful, they must anticipate the vengeance of the evil spirits. Once they have recaptured the lost soul, they bring it back and restore it to the deprived body, thus achieving the cure.[45]

Anachronistically, we can call the approach Kierkegaardian. The ritual deals with subjectivity, the social context, and is teleological.

The psychologists I have considered also exemplify the Kierkegaardian approach, which I shall hence explore in more detail. First, existential psychology acknowledges that we have selves, and employs subjective techniques such as empathy. Mendelson optimistically illustrates the orientation:

> If the doctor has enthusiasm and hope, and can communicate this to the patient, then the patient is going to feel better. A healer is a healer no matter what techniques he uses...As the failure of psychiatric chemotherapy, psycho-surgery, electroshock therapy, analysis and most counselling is exposed—in favour of strong familial, friendship, self-esteem support networks—most of psychiatry will disappear.[46]

We are advised to temper our enthusiasm for reductive approaches to mental illness since they often contain, for instance, an epistemological ambiguity. Suffice it to say that it is reasonable to think that both physiology and the social context—the patient's private, family, and societal situation—need to be taken into account (and decisions for therapy undertaken on a strict case-by-case basis).

Second, the notion that some forms of social organization are illegitimate—because they are at odds with human nature—is implicit in the social critique of, for example, Durkheim, Illich, Hillman, Szasz, Adler, Binswanger, May, and Laing. As Illich puts it:

> For more than a century, analysis of disease trends has shown that the
> environment is the primary determinant of the state of general health of
> any population...An advanced industrial society is sick-making because it
> disables people from coping with their environment and, when they break
> down, it substitutes a clinical prosthesis for the broken relationships.[47]

Adler, Binswanger, May, and Laing emphasize the social context, which is
consistent with the limiting factors for human flourishing discussed in chapters
6 and 8. They also emphasize choice, which was an important variable in
Kierkegaard's thought (chapter 4).

Finally, existential psychiatrists have configured the psychiatric situation—with
an eye to the soul's *telos*—in ethical terms. A Kierkegaardian theory of the self,
which finds its exegetical culmination in chapter 8, with Winnicott, is assumed
in the practice of existential psychiatrists.

Also, the historical relevance of a key Kierkegaardian theme is extended by
considering some remarks by Sartre. Generally, many modern people suffer
from feelings of not belonging, uprootedness, and homelessness, which are
expressed as existential truths by writers of post–Second World War Europe.[48]
Sartre writes, for instance, "I want to leave, to go some place where I will be
really in my own niche, where I will fit in...But my place is nowhere; I am
unwanted, *de trop*."[49] Sartre turns an interpretation of modern science into
existential truth: "Every existing thing is born without reason, prolongs itself
out of weakness and dies by chance."[50] For Sartre, human actions consequently
often express a desire to be God. What Sartre means is that we desire to be
complete and not lacking in any respect (God stands for the idea of this most
perfect being, as that which is complete unto itself).

We may, for example, attempt to achieve fulfilment by belonging to something
beyond ourselves.[51] Consider the words of A. Maslow, in discussing the mystic
as attaining a feeling of belonging:

> It is quite characteristic that the whole universe is perceived as an
> integrated and unified whole...that the universe is all of a piece and that
> one has one's place in it—one is part of it, one belongs to it.[52]

As Carl Jung noted in his practice:

> Among all my patients in the second half of life—that is to say over thirty-
> five—there has not been one whose problem in the last resort was not
> that of finding a religious outlook on life. It is safe to say that every one
> of them fell ill because he had lost that which the living religions of every
> age have given their followers, and none of them has been really healed
> who did not regain this religious outlook. This of course has nothing to
> do with a particular creed or membership of a church.[53]

I have, in this study, considered two ways in which the desire to belong can
be expressed: theologically, where we seek a relationship to God, and socially,
where we attempt to be well integrated in a human community.[54]

Since Kierkegaard's theory has had wide influence, even if not always acknowledged, it was desirable to review the results. In this chapter, we considered several key existential psychiatrists who relied upon Kierkegaard's theory of self in practice, as well as Sartre. In the next chapter, I present my conclusions.

⊱ 12 ⊰

THE SELF
ACCORDING TO KIERKEGAARD

IT IS NECESSARY to understand both my conclusions and how I arrived at them. We shall thus retrace our steps and summarize the findings. I shall provide a brief overview of the different ways the self has been configured in my study. Finally, I will roughly highlight the benefits of viewing the self along the lines of Kierkegaard.

KIERKEGAARD REVISITED
This study took its beginning by considering Kierkegaard's theological conception of the self. Kierkegaard felt selfhood culminated in a God-relationship, legitimating his ascetic lifestyle and providing the solution to the despair he felt. I have attempted to demonstrate that Kierkegaard does have a concept of human nature (which we can fulfil or not). His teleological account is generically Aristotelian.

In the second part, I considered an alternative view—shared to some extent by Rousseau, Durkheim, and Winnicott—in order to develop a contrast to and emendation of Kierkegaard's account. This sociological model locates the essential notion of belonging in the human world. Fulfilment is found by being well integrated into society. I have traced how, historically, the theology of the self slowly receded, giving way to a discourse of functionality with Durkheim and (to a lesser extent) Winnicott.

Furthermore, when reason displaces God, cultural relativism can be consumed as anthropological fact. Ironically, the enlightened intellectual's emphasis upon reason led to the destruction of objectivity. The thinkers considered, however, had implicitly attempted to immunize themselves to the threat of cultural relativism with their social critique, which presupposed a conception of human nature. It is unclear, however, if this sociological conception of human nature is robust enough to stave off cultural relativism. For Kierkegaard, on the other hand, relativism is ruled out; not all ways of being are as good as any other.

I have made a point of only considering authors who can be categorized as having followed the romantic tradition. For instance, the notion that the theological writings of Kierkegaard and those of the sociologists can both be located within the romantic tradition—in terms of the emphasis upon subjectivity, a social critique, and teleology—shows how heterogeneous the reactions to the Enlightenment were. The romantics, in fact, can complement the Enlightenment in different ways, as the various theories of the self I considered demonstrate.

The theological and sociological conceptions of the self seem to terminate in different places. The eschatology of the self terminates in a radical individuality for Kierkegaard, and in social relations for the sociologist (such as Durkheim).

I have also pointed out there are also commonalities between Kierkegaard and the sociological school. I have suggested that we can utilize Winnicott's concept of interdependence to reconcile the romantics' dilemma—that of being torn between complete isolation, which, after all, does not seem the healthiest route to the fulfilment of human nature—and the hypocrisy that seems to inevitably arise within social groups. The concept of interdependence, it is important to note, is consistent with Kierkegaard's idea that we have to be alone with God in order to find the ground of ethics. The concept of interdependence also captures the sociologists' emphasis upon the social context without annulling autonomy. A virtue of this study is that I have attempted to contribute to clarity within the romantic tradition, whose proponents are often torn between a radical individualism and a desire for community. The convergence of the theological and sociological accounts of the self provides the basis for discussing consequences for the two schools collectively.

As noted in the introduction, in utilizing sociological thinkers to complement Kierkegaard's thought, I do not render a verdict on the importance of relating one's self to a concept of eternity. In the present context, there is more to be gained from stressing commonalities than differences. Suffice it to say that the sociological concept of the self takes on a different hue (not a different colour). A relationship to eternity is not inconsistent, for example, with the Kierkegaardian conception of the self where our social nature is emphasized.

In the part called *Some Consequences for Practice*, not to overlook differences, I remark upon the diverse historical consequences of adopting a theological or sociological conception of the self. In chapter 9, for instance, I show that suicide has been viewed as a moral issue (under Christian regimes) and a social one (in societies operating under scientific mores). In chapters 10 and 11, however, by considering the thought of Adler, Binswanger, May and Laing, I attempted to demonstrate that there can be uniform consequences for practice from following a generically Kierkegaardian approach.

I have three conclusions about a Kierkegaardian conception of the self.

(a) Kierkegaard's emphasis on **subjectivity** entails that reductionism can never comprise the whole story about what we are. The Kierkegaardian notion of the self developed here aims to outline a structure of the self. We understand ourselves in relation to time (the possible and necessary) and for Kierkegaard, in the end, in relation to eternity (the impossible or absurd). Kierkegaard's account of the structure of the self preceded, and likely contributed to, the contemporary and powerful metaphor of the self as a narrative; like a good story, we all have a past, a present, and a future, as well as a motivating problem and solution.

(b) Following on the heels of the previous point, the **social world** provides the backdrop of the Kierkegaardian self. Necessity and possibility only make sense in a social context. Social life is a prerequisite for selfhood. Possibility is also mediated through (though not fully determined by) the fulfilment of social prerequisites.[1] Community (an equitable one), understood generally, is a vehicle for becoming a person, and a context in which to find fulfilment. Even Kierkegaard's relationship to God terminates in a man–God–man nexus. The social aspect of selfhood is never annulled.

(c) Finally, the Kierkegaardian self is **teleological**. Our nature, for the Kierkegaardian, transcends history. Though we can be configured differently, there are, it is plausible to think, basic requirements in any social organization that must be fulfilled. According to Kierkegaard, for example, we must choose to submit to God's will in order to come into our own.[2] For those of a secular persuasion, like many romantics, "submitting to God's will" can be understood as believing that there is a way things are meant to be, and striving to achieve that.

It is worth noting that the type of *telos* that I have emphasized in the Kierkegaardian account is structural in a specific way. For example, we could say that human beings have language or a desire to belong. Many different social organizations, hence ways of constructing selves, however, are consistent with structural invariables of such generality. Cultural relativism looms large. Further elucidation or argument may be required to substantiate the moral realism hinted at by the romantics. For Kierkegaard and the other romantics, an account of the self was intended to be the cornerstone of ethical and social governance.

This study increases our historical appreciation of the role Kierkegaard's theory of the self has played in the genesis of related philosophical ideas, and, more generally, of his work as a statement of Romanticism. Also, it forces us to reflect on the etiology of mental illness as partly a social problem.

In this chapter we retraced our steps, summarizing the findings. A great deal of ground has been covered along what may seem like a path both winding and twisting. Perhaps the path to discovery could not be otherwise.

NOTES

NOTES TO SEARCH FOR THE KIERKEGAARDIAN SELF

1. Brook and Stainton distinguish between the strongest naturalism and its weaker varieties (2000, 192–3). My object of concern is the strongest naturalism as it requires an elimination of the self, whereas, for example, a moderate naturalism is nothing more than the idea that the philosophy of knowledge and language should be *informed about* what empirical scientists have discovered about knowledge and mind. It is assumed that one of the weaker forms of naturalism is consistent with a Kierkegaardian theory of the self.
2. For my purposes, the age of reason is the time of the machine.
3. Pence 2000, 20.
4. G. Pence defines cultural relativism as "the ethical theory that moral evaluation is rooted in and cannot be separated from the experience, beliefs and behaviours of a particular culture, and hence, that what is wrong in one culture may not be so in another" (2000, 12).
5. I have chosen to use the terms "self" and "soul" interchangeably because neither one offers any more precision than the other, and, in my usage, they refer to the same thing.
6. For an overview consult, for example, Block et al. 2003, *The nature of consciousness*, parts 6 and 7. Also see: Thagard 1996; Levitin 2002; Perry 2003. For a defence of reductionism, see Kim 2000 (or Churchland in Block 2003).
7. Robinson 1968, *An introduction to early Greek philosophy*, 5.64.

NOTES TO STRUCTURE OF THE SELF

1. Kierkegaard 1989, *Sickness unto death: A Christian psychological exposition for edification and awakening*, 43.
2. Ibid., 43.
3. Ibid., 43.
4. Ibid., 61.
5. Ibid., 62–3. When we speak of losing ourselves, it is hard not to recall the chilling story by Dostoevsky, *The Double*, in which someone is replaced by a double, yet no one notices except the person who has been "replaced."
6. The idea is already present in Hegel 1977, *Phenomenology of spirit*, 12.
7. Kierkegaard 1989, 43. The three cases I draw upon are all found on this page.
8. Ibid., 53.
9. Ibid., 55.
10. Ibid., 48.

11. Ibid.
12. Ibid., 49.
13. Ibid., 50.
14. Ibid., 51.
15. Ibid., 44.
16. Kierkegaard 1989, *Sickness unto death*, 44.
17. Ibid., 45
18. Ibid.
19. Ibid., 46.
20. Ibid., 47.
21. I can choose to be a sailor, a philosopher, a mathematician, in the narrow sense that I can do what it takes to be these things. But to become these things requires interest, and this is not something I can choose. I cannot choose to be interested in sailing, philosophy, or mathematics. Kierkegaard thinks that we know that we have found our vocation not by being good at it but by being able to practise it, which, let us admit, takes interest (Kierkegaard 1938, *Purity of heart*, 187).
22. "Rebelling against all existence, it thinks it has acquired the evidence against existence, against its goodness. The one in despair thinks that he himself is the evidence. And it is this that he wants to be; this is the reason he wants to be himself, to be himself in his agony, so as to protest with this agony against all existence." When one is in despair, and thinks all the world "a mess," one perhaps wants to be oneself just to evidence the dis-order of things. Anti-Climacus speaks of "the sin of writing instead of being, the sin of relating ourselves in imagination to the good and true instead of being it, or rather, of striving existentially to be it" (Kierkegaard 1989, 109).
23. Kierkegaard 1989, 52.
24. Ibid., 55.
25. Ibid., 58.
26. Ibid., 59.
27. Ibid., 60.
28. Ibid., 67.
29. Ibid., 63–4.
30. Ibid., 65.
31. Ibid., 66.
32. Ibid., 68.
33. Ibid., 69.
34. Ibid., 70.
35. Anti-Climacus accuses the petty bourgeois of having no imagination or soul, of thinking only in the infantile terms of causal connections and probabilities. "For the petty bourgeois thinks he is in control of possibility, has lured this tremendous elasticist into the snare, or madhouse, of probabilities, thinks he holds it prisoner. He carries possibility about captive in the cage of probability..." The idea of possibility, linked to its metaphysical goal—becoming ourselves—is reduced by the petty bourgeois to some secular game of probabilities, where he parades it with his pseudo-sophistication. The very meaning of possibility is beguiled by its reduction to probabilities (ibid., 72) .
36. Ibid., 86.
37. What being ourselves amounts to is given, in part, in a description of solitude: "He not infrequently feels the need of solitude; it is a necessity of life for him,

sometimes like breathing, sometimes like sleep. Now the fact that it is more of a necessity for him than for others is also a sign that he has a deeper nature. In general, the urge for solitude is a sign that there is after all spirit in a person and the measure of what spirit there is." (Ibid., 95)

38. Kierkegaard 1962, *Works of love*, 253.

NOTES TO SELF-BECOMING

1. Kierkegaard's remarks about non-Christian philosophy, which he is happy to call "paganism," is almost always referred to despairingly. He engages in a polemic that results in non-Christians becoming synonymous with the "bad." Notwithstanding Kierkegaard's determinedly Christian perspective, he finds the need to have some sympathy with the Greeks; after all, in Kierkegaard's mind, Socrates was almost a precursor to the modern-day Christian martyr.
2. Kierkegaard 1989, *Sickness unto death*, 52. The symbolic role women play for Kierkegaard will become important to understanding the idea of the religious phase of human development.
3. Ibid., 29.
4. Ibid., 128.
5. Ibid., 135. Once a girl said to me, "I know I am going to be an artist, it is the only way I know how to be at peace." This is an example of finding our vocation in life, our calling.
6. Ibid., 141.
7. Ibid., 143.
8. Kierkegaard 1980, *The concept of anxiety*, 9.
9. Ibid., 14.
10. Kierkegaard 1987b, 206.
11. Ibid., 207.
12. Kierkegaard 1980, 77.
13. Ibid., 42.
14. Ibid., 49.
15. Kierkegaard 1980, 61.
16. Ibid., 56–7.
17. Ibid., 87.
18. Ibid., 155.
19. Ibid., 158.
20. Kierkegaard 1980, 53.
21. Ibid., 74. Kierkegaard also allows for anxiety over the good, but he calls this "the demonic" (ibid., 119). In this case, anxiety is not aiding human development as it is keeping us from "the good."
22. Ibid., 129.
23. Ibid., 130.
24. Ibid., 132.
25. Ibid., 138.
26. Ibid.
27. Ibid.
28. Ibid., 142.
29. Ibid., 143.
30. Ibid., 142.
31. Ibid., 147.
32. Ibid., 150.

33. Ibid., 151.
34. Kierkegaard 1987b, *Either/or II*, 311.
35. Kierkegaard 1987a, *Either/or I*, 207. There are also comments on women in *Stages on life's way*, 57.
36. Kierkegaard 1987a, 68.
37. Sculpture captures human beauty, while painting depicts celestially transfigured beauty (ibid., 70).
38. Ibid., 19. Since the aesthetic stage is something to be overcome, it is not surprising that Kierkegaard views it disparagingly. As a philosopher, he seems to respect that being preoccupied with the sensual world is part of human development, most likely youth. He looks upon those who are in this phase of development as a father does a child who is "figuring things out for himself," with compassion. We can put it like this. He himself recognizes the vanity of finding our foundation within the temporal world, yet does not feel any malice toward those who live in that manner.
39. Kierkegaard 1987b, 248.
40. Kierkegaard 1987a, 155.
41. Kierkegaard 1987a, 305.
42. Kierkegaard 1987a, 222. (We could see similarities with the Buddhist notion of desire or the Freudian child driven solely by the pleasure principle.)
43. Kierkegaard 1990, *Eighteen upbuilding discourses*, 84.
44. Ibid., 76.
45. Ibid., 101.
46. Romans 8.6 (NKJV). Hereafter, all scripture passages are taken from the NKJV.
47. Psalms 144:4; 39:5–6.
48. Kierkegaard 1987a, 367.
49. Kierkegaard 1987b, 179.
50. Ibid., 133.
51. Ibid., 146.
52. Kierkegaard 1987a, 400.
53. Ibid., 250.
54. Ibid., 256.
55. Ibid., 274.
56. Kierkegaard 1988, *Stages on life's way*, 153.
57. Kierkegaard 1987b, 292.
58. Ibid., 282.
59. Ibid., 240.
60. Robinson 1968, *An introduction to early Greek philosophy*, 5.63.

NOTES TO THE GOD-RELATIONSHIP

1. Kierkegaard 1983, Supplement, *Fear and trembling*, 248.
2. Kierkegaard 1983, *Fear and trembling*, 12–13.
3. Kierkegaard 1991, *Practice in Christianity*, 18.
4. Kierkegaard 1983, *Fear and trembling*, 18.
5. Ibid., 37.
6. Ibid., 43.
7. Ibid.
8. Ibid., 55.
9. Kierkegaard 1989, *Sickness unto death*, 154.

10. Kierkegaard 1983, *Fear and trembling*, 62. Kierkegaard writes, "If the one who is to act wants to judge himself by the result, he will never begin" (62–3).

11. Ibid., 69.

12. Kierkegaard 1988, *Stages on life's way*, 384.

13. Kierkegaard 1985, *Philosophical fragments*, 51.

14. Ibid., 74.

15. Ibid., 75.

16. Kierkegaard 1983, *Fear and trembling*, 78.

17. Ibid., 80.

18. The word itself can be very misleading, and has, as a matter of fact, given rise to misinterpretation, such as Heiberg's formulation. There is some textual evidence present where Kierkegaard speaks of repetition in relation to nature.

19. Ibid., 132.

20. Ibid., 322.

21. Ibid., 133.

22. Ibid., 186.

23. Ibid., 306.

24. Ibid., 315.

25. Ibid., 313.

26. Kierkegaard 1983, *Fear and trembling/repetition*, 201.

27. Ibid., 326–7.

28. Kierkegaard 1989, *Sickness unto death*, 228.

29. Ibid., 220.

30. Psalms 52:5.

31. Kierkegaard 1989, 222.

32. Ibid., 230.

33. Kierkegaard 1987b, 162.

34. Kierkegaard 1987b, 160.

35. Ibid., 188–9.

36. Kierkegaard 1988, *Stages on life's way*, 269.

37. Kierkegaard 1990, *Eighteen upbuilding discourses*.

38. Ibid., 19.

39. Ibid., 27.

40. Ibid., 24.

41. Ibid., 162.

42. Ibid., 192.

43. Ibid., 110.

44. Kierkegaard 1990, *Eighteen upbuilding discourses*: "Let us praise what is truly praise worthy, the glory of human nature" (182).

45. Ibid., 187.

46. Ibid., 191.

47. Ibid., 215.

48. Ibid., 226.

49. Ibid., 241.

50. Ibid., 307.

51. Ibid., 309.

52. Ibid., 319.

53. Ibid., 314.

54. Ibid., 321.

55. Ibid., 325.
56. Ibid., 328.
57. Ibid., 382.
58. Ibid., 400.
59. Kierkegaard 1992, *Concluding unscientific postscript to philosophical fragments*, 121.
60. Kierkegaard 1988, *Stages on life's way*, 437.
61. Ibid., 430.
62. Kierkegaard, 1990 supplement, *Eighteen upbuilding discourses*, 484.
63. Kierkegaard 1962, *Works of love*.
64. Ibid., 61.
65. Ibid., 339.
66. Ibid., 113.
67. Ibid., 153.
68. Ibid., 158.
69. Ibid., 181.
70. Ibid., 208.
71. Ibid., 111.
72. Ibid., 151.
73. Ibid., 148.
74. Ibid., 150.
75. Ibid., 151.
76. Ibid., 187.
77. Ibid., 257.
78. Ibid., 259.
79. Kierkegaard 1938, *Purity of heart*, 38.
80. Ibid., 10.
81. Ibid., 59.
82. Kierkegaard 1962, *Works of love*, 352.
83. Ibid., 352.
84. Ibid., 213.
85. Ibid., 247.
86. Ibid., 251.
87. James 2:22.
88. John 1:4–12. Also, of course, Romans: "You shall love your neighbour as yourself" (Romans 13:9).

Notes to Self and Knowledge

1.   Kierkegaard 1987b, *Either/or II*, 361.
2.   Ibid., 361.
3.   Kierkegaard 1990, *Eighteen upbuilding discourses*, 233.
4.   Kierkegaard 1983, *Fear and trembling*, 121.
5.   Kierkegaard 1992, *Concluding unscientific postscript to philosophical fragments*, 451.
6.   Ibid., 40.
7.   Kierkegaard 1992, *Concluding unscientific postscript to philosophical fragments*, 34.
8.   Ibid., 80.
9.   Kierkegaard 1989, *Sickness unto death*, 151.
10. Kierkegaard 1985, *Philosophical fragments*, 1.

11. Kierkegaard 1985, 5.
12. Ibid., 13.
13. Ibid., 37.
14. Ibid., 96.
15. Ibid., 132.
16. Ibid., 149. Kierkegaard recognizes two or three types of knowledge. Sometimes the distinction is between historical knowledge and philosophical knowledge, and at other times there is the taxonomy of absolute, objective, and subjective knowledge.
17. Ibid., 159.
18. James 1:6.
19. Kierkegaard 1992, 93.
20. Kierkegaard 1985, *Philosophical fragments*, 169.
21. Ibid., 168.
22. Kierkegaard 1985, Supplement, 255.
23. Kierkegaard 1992, 135.
24. Ibid., 308.
25. Ibid., 347.
26. Ibid., 309.
27. Ibid., 331.
28. Ibid., 309.
29. Kierkegaard 1985, 169.
30. Kierkegaard 1992, 312.
31. Ibid., 331.
32. Kierkegaard 1985, 171.
33. Ibid., 259.
34. Kierkegaard 1992, 123.
35. Ibid., 118.
36. Ibid., 244.
37. Ibid., 149.
38. Kierkegaard 1985, 165.
39. Kierkegaard 1992, 183.
40. Ibid., 203–4.
41. Ibid., 209.
42. Ibid., 263.
43. Ibid., 254.
44. Ibid., 262.
45. Ibid., 282.
46. Ibid., 265.
47. Ibid., 278.
48. Ibid., 303.
49. Ibid., 397. Kierkegaard is cognizant of how unpopular asceticism is in the secular world. For example, he says that today a man would be regarded as a lunatic if he were to enter a monastery (which, he adds, resembles an asylum in many ways). Although he goes on to say it is "encouraging" to be regarded as mad (an idea coherent with Kierkegaard's value upon being the outsider).
50. Ibid., 351.
51. Ibid., 428.
52. Ibid., 506.

Notes to Reflections and Appraisals

1. Kierkegaard 1987b, *Either/or II: A fragment of life*, 362.
2. Kierkegaard 1989, *Sickness unto death*, 35.
3. Kierkegaard 1991, Supplement, *Practice in Christianity*, 280.
4. Ibid., 280–1.
5. Ibid., 293.
6. Ibid., 336.
7. Kierkegaard 1938, *Purity of heart*, 143.
8. Kierkegaard 1985, *Philosophical fragments*, 119–29.
9. Kierkegaard 1985, Supplement, *Philosophical fragments*, 239.
10. Kierkegaard 1991, Supplement, *Practice in Christianity*, 291.
11. Thompson 1973, *Kierkegaard*, 8.
12. Ibid., 116.
13. Kierkegaard 1980, Supplement, *Concept of anxiety*, 170.
14. Ibid., 171.
15. Kierkegaard 1985, Supplement, *Philosophical fragments*, 239.
16. Kierkegaard 1987a, Supplement, *Either/or I*, 510.
17. Kierkegaard 1985, Supplement, *Philosophical fragments*, 184.
18. Kierkegaard 1987b, Supplement, *Either/or II*, 517.
19. Ibid., 521.
20. Ibid., 525.
21. Kierkegaard 1980, Supplement, *The concept of anxiety*, 170.
22. Ibid., 172.
23. Kierkegaard 1992, 185. Also see 1980, 7.
24. Kierkegaard 1985, Supplement, *Philosophical fragments*, 223.
25. Ibid., 224.
26. Ibid.
27. Ibid., 225.
28. Kierkegaard 1987b, Supplement, *Either/or II*, 438.
29. Kierkegaard 1990, Supplement, *Eighteen upbuilding discourses*, 489.
30. For example, we can look to the first page of the preface in *Either/or I*.
31. Kierkegaard 1987b, Supplement, *Either/or II*, 445. This theme is also found in *The point of view as my work as an Author*, and *Eighteen upbuilding discourses*. Note, in both these works his writing is under his own name to confront the reader directly.
32. Kierkegaard 1990, Supplement, *Eighteen upbuilding discourses*, 482.
33. Kierkegaard 1980, Supplement, *The concept of anxiety*, 191.
34. This is from the historical introduction in *Concept of anxiety*, edited and translated by R. Thomte in collaboration with A. B. Anderson 1980, xiv.
35. Kierkegaard 1991, *Practice in Christianity*, 90, 91.
36. Ibid., 92.
37. Kierkegaard 1991, Supplement, *Practice in Christianity*, 358.
38. Kierkegaard 1940, *The present age*, 3.
39. Ibid., 3.
40. Ibid., 60.
41. He sees reflection as a modern malady: "Its condition is that of a man who has only fallen asleep towards morning: first of all come great dreams, then a feeling of laziness, and finally a witty or clever excuse for remaining in bed" (ibid., 4).
42. Ibid., 48.

43. Ibid., 6.
44. Ibid., 38.
45. The creation of mass society changes our ability, according to him, to act "on principle" (ibid., 54).

NOTES TO ROUSSEAU

1. Rousseau 1993, *Émile*, 36.
2. Ibid., 11.
3. Ibid., 24–5.
4. Ibid., 27. He also remarks that great needs spring from great wealth; often the best way to get what we need is to get rid of what we have (ibid., 53).
5. Ibid., 525.
6. Rousseau 1966, Essay on the origin of languages, in J. Mortan and A. Gode, *On the origin of language*, 68. Poetry is mentioned on this page. In his value system it represents an almost nostalgic mystical form of communication as it is believed to have origins in the beginning of language and thought.
7. Ibid., 68.
8. Ibid., 5. He claims it is language that distinguishes man from the animals.
9. Rousseau 1989b, The second discourse, in J. M. Porter, *Classics in political philosophy* (ed.) 1989, 347.
10. Rousseau 1966, *Essay on the origin of languages*, 5.
11. Ibid., 10.
12. Ibid., 12.
13. Ibid., 11.
14. Ibid., 17.
15. Ibid., 13.
16. Rousseau 1993, *Émile*, 7.
17. Rousseau 1989a, 342.
18. Rousseau 1993, 218.
19. Ibid., 53.
20. Ibid., 56–7. In becoming men and women we are said to become carefree, as in no longer being treated as dependent infants.
21. Ibid., 58.
22. Rousseau 1989a, The second discourse, 338.
23. Ibid., 339.
24. Ibid., 349.
25. Rousseau 1989b, The social contract, in J. M. Porter (ed.) 1989, 357.
26. Ibid., 359.
27. Ibid., 362.
28. Ibid., 374.
29. Ibid., 360.
30. Ibid., 378.
31. Ibid., 370.
32. Ibid., 373.
33. Rousseau 1993, 332.
34. Ibid., 510–11.
35. Ibid., 5.
36. Ibid., 2.
37. Ibid., 10.
38. Ibid., 204.

39. Ibid., 210.
40. Rousseau 1966, 45.
41. Rousseau 1993, 303.
42. Ibid., 304.
43. Ibid., 301.
44. Ibid., 305. He maintains a healthy distrust of instrumental reason: "small minds have a mania for reasoning..." (341).
45. He writes, "Émile is not made to live alone, he is a member of society, and must fulfil his duties as such. He is made to live among his fellow men and he must get to know them. He knows mankind in general; he has still to learn to know individual men" (ibid., 349).
46. Ibid., 523.
47. Durkheim 1960, *Montesquieu and Rousseau*, 66.
48. Rousseau 1993, 78. New needs are born in the civil state, which have consequences such as competition and war. Whereas in the natural state man had all he needed.
49. Durkheim 1960, 89.
50. Ibid., 90.
51. Ibid., 116.
52. According to Taylor, politics guaranteed individual rights. Conversely, recognition of others was traditionally a cultural issue. An individual psychology buttresses liberalism and social psychology communitarians, says Taylor. In liberalism, everyone is equal and granted the same rights as others. A social psychology, however, recognizes that to even become ourselves we need more than just the basic human rights, as traditionally understood by liberals, but also a community or culture, and may make it more important to protect group rights.
53. Taylor 1992, *The politics of recognition*, 48.
54. Aristotle also puts requirements on being ethical in *Nichomachean ethics*, 1099b.

NOTES TO DURKHEIM

1. Durkheim 1984, *The division of labour in society*, 123.
2. Ibid., 187. Scepticism over progress, 186; 190–1. Also, his argument that the division of labour reduces competition because people have different jobs is questionable, because the types of jobs in question require less skill thus allowing for expendability and, hence, more competition.
3. Ibid., 4.
4. Ibid., 33.
5. Ibid., 332.
6. Durkheim 1984, 287.
7. Ibid., 287.
8. Durkheim 1951, *Suicide*, 38.
9. Ibid., 310.
10. Ibid., 319.
11. Durkheim 1984, 302.
12. Durkheim 1965, 29.
13. Durkheim 1984, 209. Durkheim distinguishes between self-love (taking care of our needs), and selfishness (we compare ourselves with others). It is natural that we should be concerned with our self-preservation. Yet, according to him,

in the social setting we crave respect and subsequently compete for it at the expense of others (which leads to selfishness).

14. Ibid., 49.
15. Durkheim 1951, 69.
16. Durkheim 1984, 151.
17. Ibid., 285.
18. Durkheim 1965, 257.
19. Ibid., 257.
20. Durkheim 1984, 340.
21. Durkheim 1965, *The elementary forms of religious life,* 31.
22. Ibid., 22.
23. Ibid., 3.
24. Durkheim offers some bad arguments centred around the idea of language to justify the social basis for collective representations. Just because two things—language and collective representations—share in a common property does not mean one is derived from the other.
25. Durkheim 1965, 15.
26. Ibid., 31.
27. Ibid., 21.
28. Ibid., 182, 193.
29. Ibid., 51.
30. Ibid., 250.
31. Ibid., 355, 366.
32. Ibid., 86.
33. Ibid., 256–7.
34. Ibid., 483.
35. Ibid., 243.
36. Ibid., 258.
37. Ibid., 487.
38. Ibid., 259.
39. Ibid., 218.
40. Ibid., 234.
41. Ibid., 469.
42. Ibid., 76.
43. Ibid., 215.
44. Ibid., 215–6. For his claim on women being closer to nature, see page 385.
45. Ibid., 170.
46. Ibid., 209.
47. Ibid., 258.
48. Thakur 1963, *The history of suicide in India.*
49. Seward 1968, *Hari-Kiri: Japanese ritual suicide,* 9.
50. Durkheim 1965, *The elementary forms of religious life,* 367.
51. Ibid., 378.
52. Ibid., 277.
53. Durkheim 1951, 300.
54. Ibid., 324.
55. Ibid., 287. The egoist, who lacks social integration, tends toward altruism in that he wants to lose himself in a social group. In each case, there is an imbalance between needs and means, where what we desire is at odds with what is possible, and the resulting consequence is suicide.

56. Ibid., 374.
57. Ibid., 375, 169.
58. Gibbs 1968, *Suicide,* 78.
59. Durkheim 1951, 382.
60. Moris 1969, *Social forces in urban suicide.*

NOTES TO WINNICOTT

1. Winnicott 1965, *The maturation process and the facilitating environment,* 93.
2. Ibid., 9.
3. Ibid., 65.
4. Winnicott 1988, *Human nature,* 1.
5. Ibid., 10.
6. Winnicott 1971, *Playing and Reality,* 66.
7. Winnicott 1965, 15.
8. Ibid., 135.
9. Ibid., 148.
10. Ibid., 144.
11. Ibid., 224.
12. Winnicott 1988, 12.
13. Winnicot 1965, 85.
14. Winnicott 1988, 80. It is interesting that Winnicott's views are secular because in Hinduism and Buddhism, it is by not seeing the world as other, by losing the individual self, that we achieve the highest type of realization.
15. Winnicott 1988, 71.
16. Winnicott 1965, 86.
17. Winnicott 1988, *Human nature,* 19.
18. Winnicott 1971, *Playing and reality,* 69.
19. Ibid., 69. Winnicott's developmental theory can be summarized as follows: (1) subject relates to object, (2) subject discovers object with the help of fantasy, (3) subject destroys object, (4) object survives destruction, (5) subject can use object. In this progression there is a movement from making the object a thing to depend upon, unto seeing it just as another object to do with as we want.
20. Winnicott 1988, *Human Nature.* He also ties to draw a tenuous link between maturity and democracy, as if his psychology could support a particular type of social organization. The reasoning is that dependence has an affinity to monarchy, paternalism, but democracy depends on individual autonomy. However, social life is too complex to allow such categorization. Many social, technological, and economic factors can shape individuals of lesser autonomy even in democratic societies. Both Rousseau and Durkheim would see the modern world, for instance, as creating individuals of lesser autonomy, in spite of democratic regimes (152).
21. Winnicott 1971, *Playing and reality,* 65.
22. Winnicott 1965, *The maturation process and the facilitating environment,* 94.
23. Winnicott 1971, *Playing and reality,* 139.
24. Winnicott 1965, 29. We may be concerned here that he misses the socio-cultural reasons that could leave us alone. But, to be charitable, he is speaking theoretically, trying to elucidate the dynamics of the self.
25. Ibid., 32.
26. Ibid., 34.
27. Ibid., 84.

28. The individual self is recognized as being beyond a full explication, however. Winnicott puts it this way: "I have tried to state the need that we have to recognize this aspect of health: the non-communicating central self, for ever immune from the reality principle, and for ever silent. Here communication is not non-verbal; it is, like music of the spheres, absolutely personal. It belongs to being alive. And in health, it is out of this that communication naturally arises." (Ibid., 192)
29. Winnicott 1971, *Playing and reality*, 139.
30. Ibid., 141.
31. Winnicott 1965, 224.
32. Mendelson writes, "If you look at almost any other system of medicine besides the Western, you'll find a heavy reliance on food. The 'food' of Modern Medicine, however, is the drug" (1979, 38).

NOTES TO THE IDEA OF SUICIDE

1. Von Hoff 1990, *From autothanasia to suicide: Self-killing in classical antiquity*, 198.
2. Ibid., 36. Hoff lists the following (but I am sceptical about some of them): Pythagoras, 82; Anaxagoras, 72; Empedokles, 60; Speusippos, 68; Diogenes, 80; Aristotle, 62; Epicurus, 71; Zeno, 72; Dionysios circa 80; and Kleanthes, 72.
3. Ibid., 136.
4. (Even utilitarian arguments were to be found in defence of suicide: suicide was the rational act of exiting life when we found it miserable.)
5. Ibid., 84.
6. Ibid., 93.
7. Ibid., 195.
8. MacDonald and Murry 1990, *Sleepless souls: Suicide in early modern England*, 16.
9. Ibid., 221.
10. Anderson 1982, *Suicide in Victorian England and Edwardian England*, 69.
11. Ibid., 70.
12. Stengel 1964, *Suicide and attempted suicide*, 43.
13. Masaryk 1970, *Suicide and the meaning of civilization*, 3.
14. Ibid., 4.
15. Ibid., 95.
16. Ibid., 112.
17. Ibid., 125.
18. Ibid., 138 and 139 respectively.
19. It has been remarked that if Durkheim had written upon stuttering, as opposed to suicide, we would have thousands of studies being conducted on stuttering.
20. Meer 1976, *Race and suicide in South Africa*.
21. Durkheim's approach, which consisted of attempting to discern patterns of suicide based on statistics, opened up a seemingly endless array of hypotheses to test. For instance, it was asked how suicide rates varied by day of the week, time of day, month, season, climate, sex, race, occupation, rural or urban residence, and any other category imaginable. Many of these types of hypotheses were understandably thrown into disrepute or yielded inconclusive results. As it was commonly held that the English were prone to suicide because of their gloomy climate, studies were conducted that showed climates much

worse than Britain resulting in significantly lower suicide rates, falsifying the notion that climate was causally linked to suicide. The essential point, however, is that many different hypotheses were proposed and tested as a way of looking for correlation between suicide rates with some discerning factor, since it was thought that if statistics varied with a correlation to some factor, perhaps this factor was the cause of the increase or decrease in the suicide rate; for sociology, the discerning factor was taken to be social integration.

22. Anderson 1982, 74.
23. There are some notable cultural cases regarding the governance of suicide that are worth keeping in mind when considering the act of suicide. For instance, Muslims who believe in the will of Allah perceive suicide as a revolt against the will of God. (Statistically, suicide is not prevalent among Muslims, but there could be many reasons for that.) Hassan 1983, *A way of dying: Suicide in Singapore*.

NOTES TO SUICIDE AND SCHIZOPHRENIA

1. Lester 1988, *The biochemical basis of suicide*, 3. The example is my own, used to illustrate my point.
2. Ibid., 4.
3. Furthermore, some have suggested that suicide is "functional" (weeding out the weakest element of society, or reducing problems of scarcity). Yet, genetic accounts offer no good explanation of why suicide rates fluctuate. One would imagine that a "suicide gene" (if there were such a thing) would make itself extinct. Also, one may wish to note that, on the anthropological model, suicide is not, in an over-all population, a sufficient factor as to have any significant bearing on resources.
4. Ibid., 85.
5. Ibid., 71. Inevitably, there are drugs that will remove different emotional states, such as depression or fear yet, if we have not located the foundational cause of the symptoms, they are likely to return when drug use is abandoned. Any supposed gain yielded by such intrusive methods may not be the result of a physical cure as much as offering a distressed person the mental "break" that may be all that is needed. Remission rates for mental illness have not shown to vary largely from one type of therapy to another, even in comparison to those who did not receive therapy at all.
6. Morris 1969, *Social forces in urban suicide*.
7. Gibbs 1968, *Suicide*. The result of the lack of progress—in the science of society—has allowed Durkheim's work to remain surprisingly contemporary. One problem that arises in tracing the etiology of suicide to the social level is that the specific social factors are themselves contingent. For instance, if we said that the "unmarried have a higher rate of suicide," this has to be qualified as the "unmarried in society X, at time T1," because the meaning of being married or unmarried varies based on time and culture. The effect of the changing meanings may alter the experience of a certain event (or non-event) for a person in a given social context. On the one hand, if the self is itself a social construction, it will not be possible to have laws regarding the self (except as relative to the self in a social context). If, on the other hand, we assumed an idea of human nature, we could say that event X would precipitate suicide (in any social context).
8. Meer 1976, *Race and suicide in South Africa*, 256.

9. Baechler 1979, *Suicides*, 50.
10. Ibid., 23.
11. Hillman 1964, *Suicide and the soul*, vii.
12. Ibid., 36.
13. Ibid., 93.
14. Ibid., vii.
15. Ibid., 170.
16. Ibid., 87.
17. Rubkin 1979, *Growing up dead*.
18. Ibid., 51.
19. Roman and Trice 1967, *Schizophrenia and the poor*, 19.
20. Ibid., 22.
21. Barham 1984, *Schizophrenia and human value*, 43.
22. Jacobs 1966, *An anthropological physiology of schizophrenia and its socio-family context*, 69.
23. Ibid., 6. Jacobs goes on to claim that the lifetime risk of developing schizophrenia is in the area of one percent (8).
24. Ibid., 68.
25. Ibid., 64.
26. Karlsson 1966, *The biological basis of schizophrenia*, vii.
27. Schulz and Kilgalen 1969, *Case studies in schizophrenia*, 209.
28. Ibid., 22.
29. Ibid., 137.
30. Ibid., 65.
31. Ibid., 96.
32. Ibid., 169.
33. Ibid., 52.
34. Barham 1984, 47.
35. Ibid., 164.
36. Ibid., 52.
37. Ibid., 1.
38. Barham and Hayward 1991, *From the mental patient to the person*.
39. Shulz and Kilgalen 1966, 260.
40. Dunham 1965, *Community and schizophrenia: An epidemiological study*, 17.
41. Karlsson 1965, 5.
42. Szasz 1974, *The myth of mental illness*, ix.
43. Ibid., ix.
44. Ibid., xiv.
45. Ibid., 262.

Notes to Existential Psychology

1. Adler 1927, *Understanding human nature*, 13.
2. Ibid., 28.
3. Ibid., 43.
4. Ibid., 26.
5. Ibid., 69. Although Adler's idea of organ inferiority has relegated him to dusty bookshelves, the moral of the idea is not well remarked upon.
6. Ibid., 42.
7. Ibid., 82.
8. Ibid., 192.

9. Adler writes, "The character of a human being is never the basis of a moral judgement, but is an index of the attitude of this human being toward his environment and of his relationship to the society in which he lives" (ibid., 189).
10. Ibid., 238.
11. Binswanger 1963, *Being-in-the-world: Selected papers of Ludwig Binswanger*, 220.
12. May 1967, *Psychology and the human dilemma*, 93.
13. Ibid., 182.
14. May 1969, *Love and will*, 295.
15. May 1977, *The meaning of anxiety*, 363.
16. May 1967, 105.
17. May 1969, 17.
18. May 1977, ix.
19. Ibid., 4.
20. Ibid., 17.
21. Ibid., 238.
22. May 1953, *Man's search for himself*, 26.
23. Ibid., 24.
24. Ibid.
25. Ibid., 14.
26. Ibid., 26.
27. Ibid., 179.
28. Laing 1960, *The divided self: An existential study of madness and sanity*, 18.
29. Ibid., 33.
30. Laing 1967, *The politics of experience and the bird of paradise*, 36.
31. Laing 1960, 34.
32. Ibid., 165.
33. Laing 1967, 20.
34. Ibid., 110.
35. Ibid., 24.
36. Laing 1960, 117.
37. Ibid., 85.
38. Ibid., 148.
39. I have put together different aspects of the different stories to make Laing's point.
40. Laing 1964, *Sanity, madness and the family*, 177.
41. Laing 1967, 95.
42. Laing says, "If a man is not two-dimensional, having a two-dimensional identity established by a conjunction of identity-for-others, and identity-for-ourselves, if he does not exist objectively as well as subjectively, but only a subjective identity, an identity-for-himself, he cannot be real." (Laing 1960, 95)
43. Psalms 102:3–7, 11.
44. Nietzsche 1954, *The gay science*, 125.
45. Ellenberger 1955, *Discovery of the unconsciousness*, 13.
46. Mendelson 1979, *Confessions of a medical heretic*, 176, 179.
47. Illich 1964, *The limits of medicine: The expropriation of health*, 25, 174.
48. *Narcotics anonymous*, 118. Though the illustrations are from an extreme corner, they do seem to articulate what Sartre (and Kierkegaard) had in mind: "Loneliness is something that I've lived for years; from the time I was a child,

people always let me know I was different" (ibid., 118). "From the time I was a little girl, I can remember feeling like I didn't really belong. I thought I must be an alien from another planet...I felt a big empty hole inside of me and I spent the next twenty years trying to fill in" (ibid. 129). From a very early age I had the intense feeling and belief that I was different" (ibid., 163).

49. Sartre 1964, *Nausea*, 172.
50. Ibid., 133.
51. Marcel 1951, *The mystery of being*, 8.
52. Lorimer 1990, 100.
53. Ibid., 1.
54. Sartre 1985, *Existentialism and human emotions*, 68.

NOTES TO THE SELF ACCORDING TO KIERKEGAARD

1. In the worst-case scenario, as noted, for example, in the Old Testament, Ecclesiastes: "Surely oppression destroys a wise man's reason" (Ecclesiastes 7:7). A society organized in a way that oppresses its people requires emendation, precisely because it frustrates the human flourishing of individuals.

2. The notion of choice resonates, optimistically, from the New Testament, Mark: "There is nothing outside the man which going into him can defile him; but the things which proceed out of the man are what defile the man" (Mark 7:15). The principle can be formalized:

$$(\alpha) \; \neg \; (Ox) \; (Ox \; \& \; Cxd) \; \& \; (Ox) \; (Ix \; \& \; Cxd)$$

x is what causes defilement: there does not exist an x outside us, but there does exist an x inside us. In order to accommodate footnote 8 (above), however, we need to allow for exceptions. Since there is no quantifier for "most" in predicate logic, the rule can be reformulated to allow for the exception referred to in Ecclesiastes:

$$(\beta) \; (Ox) \; ((Ox \; v \; Ix) \; \& \; Cxd)$$

That is, there exists an x outside or inside us and x causes defilement.

References

Adler, A. 1927. *Understanding human nature*. Walter Wolfe, trans., N.Y.: Garden City.

Anderson, O. 1982. *Suicide in Victorian England and Edwardian England*. Oxford: Clarendon.

Baechler, J. 1979. *Suicides*. Oxford: Blackwell.

Barham, P. 1984. *Schizophrenia and human value*. N.Y.: Blackwell.

———. 1991. *From the mental patient to the person*. N.Y.: Routledge.

Binswanger, L. 1963. *Being-in-the-world: Selected papers of Ludwig Binswanger*. J. Needleman, trans., N.Y.: Basic Books.

Block, N., O. J. Flanagen, and G. Güzeldere, eds. 1997. *The nature of consciousness*. Cambridge, MA: MIT Press.

Bosselman, B. C. 1958. *Self-Destruction: A study of the suicidal impulse*. Springfield, Ill: Charles C. Thomas.

Brook, A. and R. Stainton. 2000. *Knowledge and mind*. Cambridge, MA: MIT.

Dunham, W. H. 1965. *Community and schizophrenia: An epidemiological study*. Detroit: Wayne State Press.

Durkheim, E. 1951. *Suicide*. Spaulding and Simpson, trans., N.Y.: Free Press.

———. 1960. *Montesquieu and Rousseau*. Ann Arbor, Mich.: University of Michigan.

———. 1965. *The elementary forms of religious life*. J. Swain, trans., N.Y.: Free Press.

———. 1984. *The division of labour in society*. W. D. Halls, trans., London: MacMillan.

Ellenberger, H. 1970. *Discovery of the unconscious*. N.Y.: Basic Books.

Elrod, J. W. 1975. *Being and existence in Kierkegaard's pseudonymous works*. Princeton, N.J.: Princeton University Press.

Foucault, M. 1965. *Madness and civilization: A history of madness in the age of reason*. N.Y.: Vintage Books.

———. 1973. *The birth of the clinic: Archaeology of medical perception*. N.Y.: Vintage Books.

Friedman, P., ed. 1967. *On suicide*. N.Y.: International Press.

Gibbs, J., ed. 1968. *Suicide*. N.Y.: Harper Row.

Hassan, R. 1983. *A way of dying: Suicides in Singapore*. N.Y.: Oxford University Press.

Hillman, J. 1964. *Suicide and the soul*. N.Y.: Harper & Row.

The Holy Bible: Containing the Old and New Testaments, *The New King James Version*. 1982. Nashville, Tenn.: Thomas Nelson Publishing.

Hotherstall, D. 1990. *History of psychology*. N.Y.: McGraw-Hill.

Illich, I. 1964. *The limits of medicine: The expropriation of health*. N.Y.: Penguin.

Jacobs, L. I. 1966. *An anthropological physiology of schizophrenia and its socio-family context*. N.Y.: Vintage Press.

Kim, J. 2000. *Mind in the physical world*. Cambridge, MA: MIT Press.

Kaufmann, W., ed. 1954. *The portable Nietzsche*. N.Y.: Penguin.

Karlsson, J. L. 1966. *The biological basis of schizophrenia*. N.Y.: Basic Books.

Kierkegaard, S. 1938. *Purity of heart*. Douglas V. Steere, trans., N.Y.: Harper Row.

———. 1940. *The present age*. Dru and Williams, trans., London: Oxford University Press.

———.1962. *Works of love*. E. Hong and H. Hong, trans., N.Y.: Torchbooks.

———. 1980. *The concept of anxiety*. E. Hong and H. Hong, trans., Princeton, N.J.: Princeton University Press.

———. 1980. Supplement. In Kierkegaard 1980.

———.1983. *Fear and trembling/repetition*. E. Hong and H. Hong, trans., Princeton, N.J.: Princeton University Press.

———.1983. Supplement. In Kierkegaard 1983.

———.1985. *Philosophical fragments*. E. Hong and H. Hong, trans., Princeton, N.J.: Princeton University Press.

———.1985. Supplement. In Kierkegaard 1985.

———.1987a. *Either/or I: A fragment of life*. E. Hong and H. Hong, trans., Princeton, N.J.: Princeton University Press.

———.1987a. Supplement. In Kierkegaard 1987a.

———.1987b. *Either/or II: A fragment of life*. E. Hong and H. Hong, trans., Princeton, N.J.: Princeton University Press.

———.1987b. Supplement. In Kierkegaard 1987b.

———.1988. *Stages on life's way*. E. Hong and H. Hong, trans., Princeton, N.J.: Princeton University Press.

———.1989. *Sickness unto death: A Christian psychological exposition for edification and awakening*. Hanny, trans., London: Penguin.

———.1990. *Eighteen upbuilding discourses*. E. Hong and H. Hong, trans., Princeton, N.J.: Princeton University Press.

———.1990. Supplement. In Kierkegaard 1990.

———.1991. *Practice in Christianity*. H. Hong and E. Hong, trans., Princeton, N.J.: Princeton University Press.

———.1991. Supplement. In Kierkegaard 1991.

———.1992. *Concluding unscientific postscript to philosophical fragments*. E. Hong and H. Hong trans., Princeton, N.J.: Princeton University Press.

Kunitz, S. 1987. *The essential Blake*. N.J.: Ecco Press.

Laing, R. D. 1960. *The divided self*. N.Y.: Penguin.

Laing, R. D. and A. Esterson. 1964. *Sanity, madness and the family*. N.Y.: Penguin.

Laing, R. D. 1967. *The politics of experience and the bird of paradise*. N.Y.: Penguin.

Lester, D. 1988. *The biochemical basis of suicide*. Springfield, Ill: Charles C. Thomas.

Levitin, D. J. 2002. *Foundations of cognitive psychology*. Cambridge, MA: MIT Press.

Lorimer, D. 1990. *Whole in one*. N.Y.: Penguin.

MacDonald, M. and T. Murry. 1990. *Sleepless souls: Suicide in early modern England*. Oxford: Clarendon.

Marcel, G. 1951. *Mystery of being*. London: Harvill Press.

Masaryk, T. G. 1970. *Suicide and the meaning of civilization*. Weist and Batson, trans., Chicago: Chicago University Press.

May, R. 1953. *Man's search for himself*. N.Y.: W. W. Norton.

———. 1969. *Love and will*. N.Y.: W. W. Norton.

———. 1977. *The meaning of anxiety*. N.Y.: W. W. Norton.

McKeon, R., ed. 1941. *The basic works of Aristotle*, N.Y.: Random House.

Meer, F. 1976. *Race and suicide in South Africa*. London: Routledge.

Mendelson, R. 1979. *Confessions of a medical heretic*. Chicago: Contemporary Books.

Motz, L. and J. Weaver 1989. *The story of physics*. N.Y.: Avon.

Morris, R. 1969. *Social forces of urban suicide*. Illinois: Dorsey Press.

Morton, J. and A. Gode, eds. and trans. 1966. *On the origin of language*. N.Y.: Frederick Ungar Pub.

Narcotics anonymous. 1988. Van Nuys, CA: World Service Office Inc.

Nietzsche, F. 1954. The gay science. In W. Kaufmann, ed. 1954.

Pence, G. 2000. *A dictionary of philosophical terms*. N.Y.: McGraw-Hill.

Perry, J. 2003. *Knowledge, possibility, consciousness*. Cambridge, MA: MIT Press.

Pink Floyd. If. *Atom heart mother*. Capital Records.

Porter, J. M. 1989. *Classics in political philosophy*. Scarborough: Prentice-Hall.

Robinson, J. M. 1968. *An introduction to early Greek philosophy*. Boston: Houghton Mifflin Company.

Roman, P., M. Trice, and M. Harrison. 1967. *Schizophrenia and the poor*. Ithica: Cornell University.

Rousseau, J. J. 1966. Essay on the origin of languages. In Morton and Gode 1966.

———. 1989a. Social contract. In Porter 1989.

———. 1989b. Second discourse. In Porter 1989.

———. 1993. *Emilé*. Foxely, trans. London: Everyman.

Rubkin, B. 1979. *Growing up dead*. Nashville, TN: Abingdon.

Sartre, J. P. 1964. *Nausea*. N.Y.: New Directions Pub.

———. 1985. *Existentialism and human emotions*. N.Y.: Carol Pub.

Seward, J. 1983. *Hari-Kiri: Japanese ritual suicide*. N.Y.: Oxford Press.

Shulz, C. G. and R. K. Kilgalen. 1966. *Case studies in schizophrenia*. Springfield, Ill: Charles C. Thomas.

Stengel, E. 1964. *Suicide and attempted suicide*. Hammondsworth, U.K.: Macgibbon and Kee.

Szasz, T. S. 1974. *The myth of mental illness*. N.Y.: Harper &Row.

Taylor, C. 1989. *Sources of the self: The making of the modern identity*. Cambridge, MA: Harvard University Press.

———. 1992. *The politics of recognition*. Princeton, N.J.: Princeton University Press.

Thagard, P. 1996. *Mind*. Cambridge, MA: MIT Press.

Thakur, U. 1963. *The history of suicide in India*. Delhi: Vriental Pub.

Theunissen, M. 1984. *The other: Studies in the social ontology of Husserl, Heidegger, Sartre, and Buber*. 1977. C. Macann, trans., Cambridge, MA: MIT Press.

Thompson, J. 1973. *Kierkegaard*. N.Y.: A. A. Knopf.

Tillich, P. 1952. *The courage to be*. New Haven: Yale University Press.

Von Hoff, A. J. L. 1990. *From autothanasia to suicide: Self-killing in classical antiquity*. N.Y.: Routledge.

Winnicott, D. W. 1965. *The maturation process and the facilitating environment*. N.Y.: International University Press.

———. 1971. *Playing and reality*. London: Tavistock Pub.

———. 1988. *Human nature*. N.Y.: Schoken Books.

Name Index